The Joys of

A GARDEN FOR YOUR BIRDS

The Joys of

A GARDEN FOR YOUR BIRDS

by Rupert Barrington

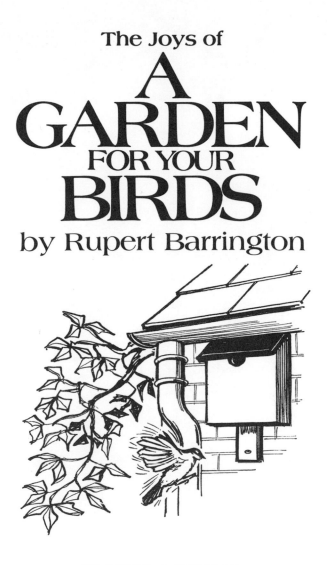

GROSSET & DUNLAP
A National General Company
Publishers   New York

Originally published in Great Britain as:

A BIRD GARDENER'S BOOK
© 1971
By Rupert Barrington

First American Edition—1972
© 1972 by Grosset & Dunlap, Inc.
All Rights Reserved
Published simultaneously in Canada
Library of Congress Catalog Card Number: 77-183026
ISBN: 0-448-01235-9

Printed in the United States of America

6 -19-73

CONTENTS

INTRODUCTION

THERE ARE THOUSANDS of gardens today which could be converted into miniature sanctuaries for birds if the right conditions were provided.

This book attempts to explain how this is done, with particular emphasis on the selection and treatment of the trees and shrubs which are most useful to garden birds. Many gardens have been planted with trees which are quite unsuitable for nesting birds, but there are also many gardens which are in the process of being planted, and it is hoped that some of the suggestions in this book will be especially helpful to those who are planning a garden and who are interested in birds.

The book is based upon observation over a period of five years on the nesting, feeding and roosting activities of birds in a large garden on the edge of a town where, owing to the large number of predators, young birds required constant protection, and where an increase both in the number and variety of garden birds was only achieved after several seasons.

Why Preserve Garden Birds?

It may well be said that there is no shortage of these birds. This is true of rural areas, but it is not true where large, treeless housing developments and industrial parks have been built. Here there are only sparrows and starlings—and as the process goes on and the countryside becomes more and more urbanized, so will the more interesting species of garden birds vanish.

Slow and creeping changes in our environment are occurring all the time. These changes are either deliberate or accidental.

A good example of a deliberate change is the situation which arises when a building contractor buys up an old Victorian house with a large garden containing many trees and shrubs in which birds have nested regularly for years. The site is bulldozed clear and perhaps thirty new houses are built on it. Each owner of a new house may have about a quarter of an acre of land where he will no doubt make a small lawn and plant a few flowers with possibly a low dividing privet hedge. His neighbor may do the same. In this way what used to be a favorite breeding ground for songbirds such as the robin, thrush, mockingbird, cardinal, goldfinch, oriole, wren, and many others, has been converted into an area in which only sparrows, starlings and a limited number of other birds which are good colonists, such as the grackle, will breed. Most of the original bird inhabitants will have to move elsewhere to find breeding grounds.

An example of an accidental change in environment is the planting of many thousands of acres with conifers for commercial use on grounds where deciduous trees and undergrowth had grown. Although this may at first seem a wonderful thing for birds, in fact it is not because conifers generally have a much poorer associated wild life than the broad-leafed trees—and this applies especially to the types of conifers which are native to the United States. Another reason is that all wood to be used commercially has to be straight, and to get trees to grow straight they must be planted very close together. Thus, when the young conifers have reached a certain stage in growth their branches are so close together that very little light can reach the ground beneath, with the result that there is no plant growth or insect life below. No ground feeding birds can live under such conditions, and the only birds which could benefit would be the relatively few which feed on the seeds or shoots of conifers. Although the latest practice is to space conifers more widely to reduce thinning costs, it is doubtful if this would allow more than a rather sparse undergrowth to grow once the trees had reached a certain height.

Naturally-occurring forests on the other hand have a very rich undergrowth of shrubs and ground-covering plants and many open spaces with grasses, brush piles and briers which have been without man's interference for hundreds of years. Such surroundings are ideal for certain species of birds, provided their privacy during the breeding season is not disturbed by the weekend invasions of picnickers, campers and hikers—something which is now happening all too often.

Dramatic and sudden changes in environment can be caused by man. A good example of this is the draining and filling of swamps near populated areas to eliminate the mosquito. Intended to affect only one species, this action has, in many cases, had a devastating and far-reaching effect on birds, fish, and wildlife in general. Often such actions may not seem harmful to larger animals, but frequently the breeding and spawning areas of tiny creatures upon which they depend for food are destroyed, thus indirectly affecting their survival in that area.

This may not seem very relevant to garden birds, but it serves to illustrate how much commercial interests have interfered with the environment of birds, and to show that nearly all types of wildlife are now under a continuous pressure. Their natural habitat is being taken away and their lives endangered.

We must try to remedy this by giving back some of the things we have taken away. This applies to all gardens, big and small, but more particularly to the newly-established garden in an area where birds have been ousted from their previous nesting places. Birds need tree and plant life to survive, and if instead of laying down concrete, labor-saving slabs we try to provide them with their natural surroundings, we are likely to be rewarded by their presence in the garden.

An English bird gardener relates the following experiences as he applied some of the bird gardening practices outlined in this book.

Having always had a great interest in birds, I usually tried to direct my gardening activities so as not to interfere with their nesting activities; but this was in a rather negative way, such as not cutting hedges till all nesting activities had stopped. It was not until I allowed a hawthorn road hedge three feet high to grow in stages up to a height of six feet (to prevent people

9

looking over) that I realized how easy it was to create nesting sites for garden birds; for in this 180 feet of hedge about six species of birds began to nest each year.

In many housing developments which I visited, I had noticed the scarcity of garden birds and the absence of suitable trees, and I decided to try out on a larger scale the idea of providing nesting sites, both natural and artificial. I was lucky enough to find a house in Cheshire, England, with a garden ideal for the purpose, because it was full of evergreens and broad-leafed trees which had not been looked after for many years, with the result that the broad-leafed trees had outgrown the evergreens, depriving them of light and stunting their growth. This presented a very good opportunity to demonstrate how medium-sized trees could be made into natural nesting sites by cutting or pruning, and how, by felling or pollarding larger trees, they could be made more useful to birds.

In the first three years everything seemed to go wrong. The existing bird population was small. There were, for example, no finches except a few greenfinches, no mistle thrushes except as winter visitors, no flycatchers, few blackbirds, and a very few thrushes. Robins, wrens and hedge sparrows were rarely seen, but predators in the form of cats, grey squirrels and magpies were everywhere.

In the fourth year, after much hard work on the trees and shrubberies, things began to take a turn for the better, and at the same time the garden had been made more predator-proof. In that year, some lesser redpolls and goldcrests appeared and nested successfully.

After a bad start, when most of the April nests were destroyed, the fifth year was most successful (the criterion of success being that the young birds were seen flying strongly with the parent birds) and species new to the garden, including chiffchaffs, blackcaps, stock doves, goldfinches, and mistle thrushes, all bred successfully. The more common garden birds, with the exception of hedge sparrows and chaffinches, all had excellent breeding seasons, judging by the number of young birds seen in August. Spotted flycatchers, for example, reared eight successful broods. Tree creepers, nuthatches, long-tailed tits and great spotted woodpeckers have not nested so far, but they are more regular visitors.

It is hoped that next season will be equally successful. In the meantime, it will be interesting to see how many extra birds there are to feed during the coming winter. On the whole the scheme has worked very well, protection from predators being the key factor in this area.

Perhaps in your area, it may be a lack of suitable nest sites, lack of water or shortage of food which prevents more birds from nesting in your garden. Look it over carefully after reading this book, taking a survey of what you have and establishing a plan for improvement. Once you implement your plan, results are almost assured.

CHAPTER ONE

Basic Requirements for Survival

BIRDS NEED TO be extremely adaptable creatures to survive a changing environment and the constant threat to their existence from enemies. Some are more adaptable than others, but even these can survive and reproduce their offspring only if the following four basic requirements are fulfilled:

(1) Suitable nesting sites (see Chapters Two, Three and Four).

(2) A regular food and water supply (see Chapter Five).

(3) Suitable roosting places (see Chapter Five).

(4) Freedom from persecution (see Chapter Six).

Each condition is as important as the other. We may put out large quantities of food for birds during the winter, but if there is nowhere for them to nest during the spring they will either go where conditions are suitable or will be unable to rear any young birds, with the result that the local bird population decreases. Similarly, if they have ideal nesting conditions but are annoyed during the breeding season, their numbers will also decrease.

These are the four conditions vital to a bird's existence and to the reproduction of its kind. To fulfill all these requirements is difficult but by no means impossible. If we can do so, birds will certainly arrive as if out of the blue and will become garden residents. There is usually no difficulty about the food supply, but the other three conditions are more difficult to achieve and it will take a little time to get the desired results. However, it will be well worth the trouble and the presence of birds in the garden will add greatly to its attraction.

Anyone who has a small suburban garden may think that birds will not come to a heavily built-up area. The answer to this is that birds of every species, except when actually nesting, are always on the look-out for suitable localities in which to live and breed. Many of our summer visitors, for example, on their way back from South America, fly in thousands right over New York and its suburbs on their way to find breeding grounds and they drop down here and there for food and water. If they find the conditions suitable, they will settle down and breed and may return again in the following year. Probably one of the best examples of bird adaptability is the way many cavity-dwellers have taken to nesting in man-made boxes. The demise of old orchards with cavity-ridden trees seemed to spell doom for the bluebird in eastern states. The fact that most home-owners in suburban areas removed damaged or diseased trees left few alternative nesting sites for these birds. But since the bluebird has accepted man-made substitute cavities, nest boxes, its population is again increasing in areas where there had been a sharp decline in numbers.

Thus we need not worry that birds object to bricks and mortar, but we do need to worry about the rapidity with which we are driving birds from their natural surroundings while not providing them with alternative accommodation suited to their needs. This gradual encroachment on the natural habitat of birds is going to continue—slowly but surely. The use of chemicals on agricultural land has come to stay. The countryside is being invaded more and more by the automobile, and the air by the airplane. Many of our rivers and lakes are no longer peaceful, but resound with the din of the speedboat or outboard motor—and this especially at the height of the breeding season. The pollution of rivers is causing national concern not, it seems, because we are particularly worried about the creatures who live in or near the rivers, but because pollution might have a damaging effect on public health. In short, the outlook for wild birds in this country is rather bleak.

Of course, some people may say why bother, birds are a nuisance in the garden, anyway. This may be true of house sparrows, but otherwise it is rather like saying that rain is a nuisance—it can be, but we could not do without it. In the same way birds do a vast amount of unseen good by consuming beetles, slugs, snails, cut-worms, mosquitos, caterpillars and a host of other insects which are garden pests.

Knowing that birds will readily adapt themselves to a new environment, we must ourselves try to create the four necessary conditions if we have a garden, for it is in such a place that we can to some extent supervise their breeding activities. As already mentioned, birds will nest close to a house if conditions are suitable, and if the occupants encourage them they will become more tame and never go very far away. Their offspring will tend to stay in the same vicinity or even in the same garden provided the numbers do not increase to such an extent that competition for food results.

The birds with which we are concerned, namely the songbirds and other small birds which normally inhabit a garden, have from very early times always nested in trees, shrubs, thick undergrowth, on steep banks and in holes in trees and cliffs. When man began to build houses, many birds such as the swallow, purple martin, sparrow and starling found that human habitations provided just the right sort of nesting environment. There was usually water nearby and waste food was often available. There was no sewage disposal, so that flies were plentiful. Corn growing and other cultivation generally made food supplies more readily available. Most important of all perhaps was that these birds found the nearness of man afforded some protection against their natural enemies in the air, the falcon, hawk and crow, and those on the ground such as the fox, weasel, skunk or the snake. Those that would not adapt to building their nests actually in man-made constructions, often nested very close to buildings in nearby trees and shrubs.

Sparrows, starlings, swallows, purple martins and swifts have benefited by the multiple nesting sites which man has provided and as a result their numbers have greatly increased. Our garden birds, with the exception of the starling and probably the sparrow, were originally woodland birds. Purple martins and swifts still nest in cliffs if there is no more suitable nesting site available. In certain areas swifts sometimes nest in tree holes. Swallows were probably cave nesters but are also supposed to have nested in hollow trees, flying in through the top, as in an old-fashioned, wide chimney, and they may even have nested on the ends of horizontal boughs.

In England, during the past 250 years, the cultivation of gardens and the Englishman's love of fencing off his property with hedges have perhaps been the main reasons why that country remained so rich in bird life for so long. The English hedge is by no means the most economical way of fencing a field, but it is certainly the most picturesque and, from a long-term agricultural point of view, by far the best way of preventing soil erosion and giving protection to the livestock. Perhaps similar practices by American farmers in the Midwest would have lessened the great losses of rich soil by erosion and dust storms during the early 1900's . . . an example of how man's unknowledgeable tampering with nature can be destructive.

In spite of recognized value, hedgerows, so important to birds, are infrequently retained. Mechanized farming is the practice and it demands that existing hedges be bulldozed out to make fields bigger and easier to farm. Hedges take time to grow and also take up space, while a barbed wire fence with concrete posts can be erected in a matter of hours and will last for many years without maintenance. It will not harbor weeds or vermin and it is a much cheaper short-term investment and a better barrier.

Birds too have a housing problem now, and if a bird cannot find a suitable nesting site at the right time its breeding efficiency will suffer considerably in that particular season. The reason for this is interesting. The egg production mechanism of most birds is not stimulated to activity unless the hen bird goes through the process of nest building. The ovulatory process seems to be stimulated by the handling of the nesting materials, and when the nest is completed egg production starts almost immediately. In the early part of the season, there is often an interval of a few days before the first egg is laid. This interval gets shorter as the season advances.

Different types of birds have different rituals in their nest building, but these rituals do not start until the building site has been decided. Many birds decide well in advance, say one or two months, where they are going to build their nest. Generally speaking, the more prolific the bird is in its breeding habits, the quicker it can decide on a new nesting site if the first nest is a failure. Again, the bigger the bird the longer it takes to choose a nesting site and the

16

more easily it is put off from breeding if anything goes amiss. The golden eagle, for example, lays only two or three eggs, and if this clutch is destroyed will probably not lay again in that season. Such birds as thrushes, blackbirds and the finch family are fortunately very persistent nest builders and will usually raise at least two broods a year, although they may have to build as many as four nests to achieve this; but here again they must be provided with appropriate nesting sites. For hygienic reasons, the majority of birds will never use the same nest again to rear a second brood, but if the old nest is pulled down the same bird may well return to exactly the same site again in the following year, or even in the same year.

If, therefore, we wish to attract birds to our garden and keep them there to breed we must try to fulfill the four requirements of suitable nesting sites, a regular food and water supply, suitable roosting places and freedom from persecution.

Feeding is perhaps the most arduous task, but it can be most rewarding when an interesting bird appears. Those who provide only winter food for birds should start when the first spell of hard weather sets in, and the feeding should be continued regularly until the weather becomes milder, usually about the end of April.

Pairing up usually takes place in the middle of February and if by feeding birds until the middle of April they can be kept in the vicinity, it is most likely that they will not go elsewhere to nest. Early nesters such as the English sparrow, mourning dove, bluebird, and robin start thinking about nesting sites quite early in March and nest building starts about the end of March. In an exceptionally mild winter, pairing takes place earlier, and the mourning dove or grackle may build in February and have young before the end of March. Starlings and English sparrows will often stake their claim on a nest box in February.

Nest boxes and other nesting devices should therefore be put up, if possible, before the middle of February, though they may be put up as late as the end of May with successful occupation by tree swallows, sparrows, wrens, or other multiple brooders.

In the breeding season, which is in full swing from mid-April till the end of July, the most important job is to keep a close watch for predators, having an occasional peep at the nest without frightening the hen bird off.

A Garden For Your Birds

The autumn is the time to think of how the existing trees and shrubs in the garden can be made more attractive as nesting sites, or to plant young trees or shrubs which can be both useful to birds for food, nesting and cover and, at the same time, are decorative to the garden.

CHAPTER TWO

Natural Nesting Sites

BIRDS MUST NECESSARILY be very particular about how and where they site their nests, and what may appear to be a good nesting site to a human may appear quite the opposite to a bird. Of course trees, shrubs and hedges may be cut or pruned to encourage nesting birds, but the effort is likely to be in vain if the site remains unsuitable. The selection of a site by a bird depends upon the following factors.

1. The Locality

Birds spend a lot of time selecting the locality in which they settle. They must be certain that a permanent food supply will be available, especially in the breeding season. A goldfinch, for example, which feeds mainly on seeding weeds, will not settle down in a locality where there are no weeds. Food supply therefore primarily determines the type of bird which will be found in a locality, but it need not be very close to the nest. Birds may fly hundreds of yards to forage or fly miles to water in winter. Indeed, as a general rule, in order not to attract attention birds do not feed in the immediate vicinity of their nests.

Water is usually available in most places, but garden birds certainly prefer to have their local drinking and bathing place near at hand, so it is best to have a birdbath in your garden.

Roosting places are not so important in the breeding season when the trees are in full leaf and the male bird roosts near his setting mate.

Birds which are incubating eggs are very liable to be disturbed at night by cats and they will therefore avoid localities where cats abound. Unaccustomed lights will cause the hen bird to fly off her nest in a panic and she will not return until morning when the eggs will be cold and infertile or the young birds, if hatched, will have died of cold. Persistent noise, such as traffic, does not deter birds from nesting provided they have become accustomed to it, but sudden unaccustomed noises or bangs will upset them.

2. Texture of Trees

The twig and branch texture is highly important. A hedge must not be too thick to allow room for a nest. Birds must be able to move about freely within a hedge or tree and the setting hen bird must be able to escape quickly if in danger. Very closely-clipped hedges do not allow birds either free entry or exit and leave no room for moving about inside. Such hedges are almost useless for birds.

Perhaps the most important feature of the texture which attracts birds is the amount of protection it affords against predators. Birds will choose a thorny tree as opposed to a non-thorny tree, to obtain protection against cats and foxes and other nest robbers. It is probable that by the process of evolution the successful breeders were those who chose thorny trees in which to nest, and so the offspring can now recognize the prickly trees by instinct rather than by the painful process of testing trees for their "thorn value."

3. Foliage

The foliage of the tree must give sufficient protection from rain and hot sun and good concealment from predators both above and below.

4. Nest Foundation

Tree-nesting birds need first of all a firm foundation which can take the weight of the nest. The foundation must have forked branches at the correct angles to support the sides of the nest. The supporting fork must not be subject to too much movement in the wind, which would loosen the nest and cause disaster. Each supporting branch in the fork must be stiff and at least a year old in growth.

5. Height of Nests

All birds have their own particular choice about the height of the nest. Tree-nesting garden birds, with a few exceptions such as the song sparrow and some of the warblers who build quite low down or on the ground, usually choose a height of 5 to 15 feet from the ground. Other exceptions are purple martins which seem to prefer artificial nesting boxes to natural sites. The martins are colonial and will nest in large, multi-celled houses which must be mounted on a 15- to 20-foot high pole in a cleared area, since these birds feed in the air and need much open space for their flight. Once established, they often return to the same site year after year. The Baltimore orioles are yet other exceptions. They sometimes build their beautifully-woven hanging nest at the extreme tip of a leafy elm or weeping willow branch, 30 to 60 feet above the ground, where it is almost impossible to see until the leaves have fallen.

The garden birds which do not use the fork structure of trees for nesting, such as cardinals, catbirds, mockingbirds, thrashers, redwinged blackbirds and chipping sparrows, often nest from 3 to 10 feet above the ground. Swallows often nest in a high, sloping bank at the water's edge or under the eaves of barns and houses.

PROVISION OF NATURAL NESTING SITES

To have birds nesting in our gardens, it is very important for us to ensure that trees are not too high and not too low and that they offer the right sort of cover at the correct height. The closely-clipped privet hedge less than 3 feet high which surrounds so many small gardens is absolutely useless for birds, being too thick, of the wrong twig texture and far too low. In many cases, however, an existing garden tree or shrub may be pruned to remedy some defect and so provide a natural nesting site.

21

Generally, most trees and shrubs are not nearly as useful to birds if allowed to grow unpruned as when they are trimmed and kept bushy. Where possible, trees must be kept at a medium height—9 to 12 feet—so that they can be kept under control by occasional pruning. Over-trimming may produce too thick a branch texture and under-trimming may have the opposite effect. It depends on the type of plant and the rate of growth of the branches. A currant, for instance, is a strong, fast grower, but if left to grow freely offers nothing much for nesting birds. If clipped lightly once or even twice a year, it can be made into a pleasant-looking, tidy shrub with plenty of nesting possibilities. Beeches, though useless as large trees, can be made into excellent nesting sites when grown as hedges.

It is necessary when trimming a hedge or tree to cut the branches in such a way that they sprout into a fork, and it is such a fork which will be chosen by tree-nesting birds. A fork should contain not less than three branches, and preferably more. The angle of the fork is important; a bird likes an angle of about 70° facing vertically upwards, allowing enough room for the nest and at the same time providing a secure fixing. If the angle faces sideways, nesting is still sometimes possible: if it is much narrower or much wider than 70°, then nesting will not be possible.

Such specialized pruning may sound too much like hard work, but if a pair of parrot-beak shears are used, suitable fork structures in, say, a hawthorn hedge, can easily be fashioned and these will be useful nesting sites for perhaps ten years. Periodic thinning inside the hedge may be necessary. This sort of pruning only applies to trees which grow branches at a suitable angle for nest building. It is a waste of time trying to make nesting sites in any tree which has a growth angle as shown in **B, C** or **D** in the drawing. It is also useless to attempt to make nesting sites in a tree which does not have a vigorous growth or a strong branch structure.

The drawings on page 24 show how a newly-planted hawthorn hedge should be grown and pruned to offer the maximum number of nesting sites for garden birds. Trees should be planted about 12 inches apart.

The method of pruning as shown should be continued until the hedge is about 6 feet high and 2 feet thick; when growth is complete the fork structure formed at a height of 4½ feet will be used as nesting sites by many garden birds.

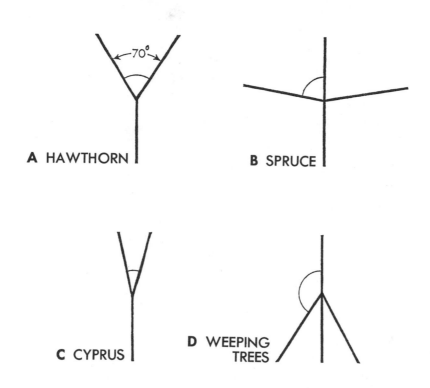

The angle of forked branches is important to tree-nesting birds. In **A** the 70° angle is ideal. **B** shows the same angle facing sideways; this might be used for nesting. The angle in **C** is too narrow, and in **D** too wide.

A nesting fork is obviously of no use to a bird if, as sometimes happens, it has a central shoot growing up the center of the fork. It is most important to remove this, otherwise no nest can be built.

NESTING POTENTIAL OF VARIOUS TREES AND SHRUBS

The trees and shrubs which are commonly found in gardens are listed below alphabetically, and comments are made as to their value

23

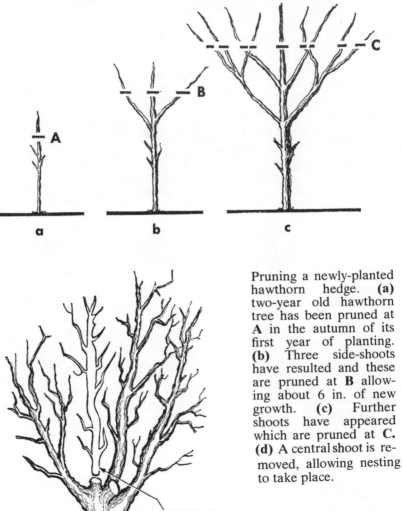

Pruning a newly-planted hawthorn hedge. **(a)** two-year old hawthorn tree has been pruned at **A** in the autumn of its first year of planting. **(b)** Three side-shoots have resulted and these are pruned at **B** allowing about 6 in. of new growth. **(c)** Further shoots have appeared which are pruned at **C**. **(d)** A central shoot is removed, allowing nesting to take place.

as nesting sites. The birds likely to nest in a particular tree are also mentioned. Many trees and shrubs have been omitted either because of their rarity or because they are obviously of no value as nesting sites. The term "free-growing" which is often used below means that a tree has never been cut back or pruned in any way. This list may seem unduly long and detailed, but our purpose is to find out why some birds seek out a particular type of tree in which to nest and why they never choose what may seem to us to be an excellent nesting site. We might look upon one leafy tree as being as good as another for nesting purposes but perching birds, whose whole life is closely dependent on trees, see the greatest difference between one tree and another, and they are very particular in their choice. To understand why this is so, it is necessary to take each of the common garden trees and shrubs in turn and to study the "pros" and "cons" of each, in relation to its value as a nesting site.

AILANTHUS

Especially good for planting in city gardens because of its ability to withstand city smoke and dust damage, the ailanthus, or Tree of Heaven, as a free-standing tree is not especially valuable to birds. Planted in masses, this plant which is fast growing, will quickly develop into a high hedge that offers far more nest sites. Birds which will build in such a hedge include song and chipping sparrows, catbirds and mockingbirds.

ANDROMEDA

This broad-leaved evergreen shrub offers limited cover and nesting sites. Those likely to use it for nesting are early-nesting robins and mourning doves or flycatchers and some warblers. Having early flowers, this shrub attracts many insects, and, in turn, insect-eating birds.

APPLE (AND PEAR)

Free-growing apple and pear trees are rarely used by nesting birds. The ruby-throated hummingbird, and orchard oriole, especially fond of tall pear trees, are exceptions.

Apple and pear trees when pruned annually and kept at a height of about 9 feet become quite thick and provide good leaf cover.

Such trees may well be used for nesting by the robin, red-eyed vireo, warbling vireo and goldfinches. If trained against a wall, blackbirds and thrushes may use them.

Where possible, old apple trees should not be completely cut down, but the branches should be lopped back leaving a stump 6 to 9 feet high. These stumps very often develop holes and cavities in which woodpeckers, bluebirds, chickadees, nuthatches, titmice and wrens show a great interest. Artificial nesting holes can be bored in them. They can also be used as a support for honeysuckle, clematis, Virginia creeper, rambling rose or climbing ivy, the latter being used also for roosting.

ARBORVITAE (SEE CONIFERS, CEDAR)

ASH

The rather common members of the ash (Fraxinus) family are of little value as nest sites due to their branch structure although a number of birds will eat their fruits. They have a thick root system which takes up much moisture from the soil and allows little but grass to grow at their feet. They are best used as isolated shade trees in a lawn area, as shrubs do not grow well near them. Old ones may be topped and used as a support for nest boxes and climbing vines.

BARBERRY

Japanese barberry, allowed to grow freely, provides nesting sites for yellow warblers, cardinals, catbirds, thrashers, thrushes, mockingbirds, vireos, song and chipping sparrows. Its thick, spiny branches afford excellent protection from cats and make it an ideal boundary hedge. Bright red berries provide emergency winter food. Scarlet autumn foliage and the ability to grow in dry soils make this one of the most widely used hedge plants.

BEECH

A large free-growing beech is very beautiful at a distance, but in a small garden it can be a nuisance and as a nesting site is of no value to garden birds. In the winter it provides beech nuts, which are popular with mourning doves, towhees, and many of the game birds.

Beech grown as a hedge can be most attractive in any garden. It

26

makes a solid boundary fence and does not require much clipping. As a nesting site it is very popular with garden birds, but the hedge should be at least 6 feet high and 2 feet thick. The thickness of all hedges is very important for nesting birds.

Goldfinches, house finches, yellowthroats, yellow warblers, catbirds and several sparrows may use beech hedges for nesting.

BIRCHES

The several varieties of birch provide nesting sites for redstarts, ruby-throated hummingbirds and vireos among their branches. Susceptible to insect damage, disease and decay, they are often favored by woodpeckers, chickadees and other insect-eating cavity-nesters both for nesting and feeding. Juncos, siskins, white-throated sparrows, titmice and finches are attracted to the birches' seeds in winter.

BITTERSWEET

Although this shrub offers little in the way of nest sites when planted alone, mixed with other shrubs to form a dense border, or used on trellises and arbors, its value is greatly improved and it will be nested in by nearly any of the birds which nest in the barberry. Although its fruits are not as popular as some, they will be eaten by bluebirds, robins, thrushes and vireos. A bittersweet vine on a trellis is an excellent place to mount a nest box or shelf.

BLACKBERRY (CULTIVATED)

A patch of cultivated blackberries at the end of a garden may attract catbirds, thrashers and mockingbirds as well as some of the small warblers. It is essential to allow weeds and grass to grow up inside the patch to give extra cover. In the autumn the growth which has fruited should be cut away, leaving only the new briars.

If grown against a wall, blackberries must be trained against trellis work as they would not by themselves give enough support for a heavy nest such as that of the thrasher.

BLACKBERRY (WILD)

Wild blackberries, as seen in open fields and woodland clearings grow into dense, impenetrable clumps which provide very safe nesting sites for cardinals, thrushes and robins, thrashers, mockingbirds and catbirds, bluebirds, orioles, grosbeaks, waxwings, white-throated, chipping and song sparrows, titmice, flickers . . . Such a formidable list should be enough to persuade any bird enthusiast to set aside a piece of unwanted garden in which to grow the common bramble.

It is necessary to trim blackberry bushes annually to keep them attractive to birds. In fields and open country, this pruning is very adequately done by cattle.

BLUEBERRY (HIGHBUSH)

This rather nicely shaped shrub is especially attractive in fall foliage and fruit—birds, too, relish its berries. Nearly a hundred species are known to eat of its fruits. Some of these are towhees, thrushes, waxwings, kingbirds, orchard orioles, titmice and game birds. Its fruits are quite edible for man as well! Song sparrows, chipping sparrows and the low-nesting warblers will set up house-keeping in it.

BOXWOOD

This tree, once so popular in Victorian gardens, is not seen very often in newly-planted gardens. It was mainly used for ornamental hedging and topiary, and as such the texture is usually too thick for birds.

If box is free-growing it will grow up to 15 feet high as a small tree and will then provide useful nesting sites for the blackbird, thrush, English sparrow, house finch, goldfinch, purple finch, chipping sparrow and some warblers.

CHERRY (FRUITING AND ORNAMENTAL)

Both types of cherry are free-growing and do not provide suffi-cient leaf cover for most garden birds except robins, kingbirds and tanagers. However, their fruits are relished by nearly all fruit-eating birds and their attractive blossoms make them a handsome addition to any garden.

CHESTNUT (HORSE)

These beautiful trees are unfortunately of very little value to garden birds, but like all large-leafed trees they do provide a great deal of shelter from heavy rain and hot sun during the summer. A goldfinch will occasionally nest in the end branches of a horse chestnut tree.

CLEMATIS

All types of clematis can be used to the advantage of birds, mainly due to the leaf cover they provide. They can be trained up trellis work or up the trunk of a dead tree or over an archway. The texture of clematis is not very strong and therefore by itself it would only support the nest of a small bird such as a goldfinch or house finch. With the support of trellis work larger birds will build in it. Some garden hybrids require annual pruning and thus are unsuitable.

CONIFERS

Some coniferous trees or shrubs are practically a necessity for any yard in order to attract a wide variety of birds. Even more important, perhaps, than for nesting and food is their function as areas of cover, especially during winter months. These plants can effectively be used, according to variety, as background plantings, hedges, border shrubs or specimen trees. Since such a variety exists, they will be grouped as follows.

Cedars and Junipers

These vary in size from low, ground-hugging shrubs to 200-foot tall trees although it is the smaller ornamental varieties that are most often planted. Birds fond of nesting in low evergreen shrubs include the myrtle warbler, house finch, song and chipping sparrows. Often found on the ground beneath such shrubs may be the nests of juncos, white-throated or fox sparrows.

Hemlocks

These flat-needled evergreens are probably best-adapted of the conifers to use as hedging as they can withstand frequent shearing. In addition to previously mentioned species, this type of hedge is attractive to catbirds, cardinals, mockingbirds, purple finches, blue jays, brown thrashers, mourning doves and several warblers. A

29

hemlock, untrimmed, grows quite tall and is attractive to other birds such as robins, thrushes, crossbills, siskins, grosbeaks, kinglets, grackles and the ruby-throated hummingbird. Winter cover is provided for game birds as well.

Pines, Spruce and Firs

Probably most valuable of the evergreens for any wildlife purpose is the white pine. Besides providing nesting sites for purple finches, pine warblers, pine siskins, crossbills, wood ducks, woodpeckers, chickadees and nuthatches, it is used for roosting by owls and grouse while bobwhites, squirrels and deer find it a food source. Many of the same birds are attracted to the other pines and various spruce and fir trees. Be sure to plant where their mature height will not be objectionable.

CRANBERRY (HIGHBUSH)

This shrub has attractive white flowers, scarlet autumn leaves and red berries which make it an excellent ornamental. It offers good cover and nest sites to any of the shrub-nesting species. Its fruits are more attractive to game birds than song birds.

CURRANT (FLOWERING)

This shrub, if kept well trimmed each year, is surprisingly useful to blackbirds and thrushes. It is a vigorous grower, seems to thrive on pruning and the twig structure is very suitable for pruning out nesting sites.

DOGWOOD

One of the most attractive of the smaller trees is the dogwood. It has a pleasing shape, showy blooms, attractive fall coloration and clusters of bright red berries. This tree is utilized for nesting by robins, cedar waxwings, flycatchers, wood pewees, vireos, goldfinches, yellow warblers, chipping sparrows and the wood thrush, but many more species including catbirds, cardinals, thrashers, thrushes, towhees, jays, kingbirds, bluebirds, grosbeaks, finches, sparrows, titmice, chickadees, nuthatches, flickers and other woodpeckers glean its autumn fruits.

There are white and pink blooming varieties which may be used as specimen trees in a lawn area, or as a background for shrubbery plantings. In addition, there are several shrub forms available including the red-twig dogwood. This rapid grower provides abundant white fruits borne on striking red stems which make it especially attractive in the winter garden. Yellow warblers and red-winged blackbirds may nest in it. The cornelian cherry is another dogwood shrub. It has small clusters of yellow flowers appearing before the leaves in the spring. Its thick foliage provides good cover and nest sites while autumn fruits attract many migratory species.

ELDERBERRY

The elder is not often seen in gardens as it is looked upon as being too much like a weed. It grows rapidly up to a considerable height. Nevertheless it is quite popular with birds even when free-growing for, though the foliage is not particularly thick, the branch angles are ideal for nest foundation and the bark, being somewhat rough, makes the nest more secure.

To improve the nesting possibility it should be pruned annually, leaving about a foot of new growth each year. In this way good nesting sites can be made especially for cardinals, thrushes, mockingbirds and thrashers.

The hollow stems of an old tree are popular with chickadees and titmice and the autumn berries of the elder are eaten by various birds including warblers, orioles, tanagers, vireos and waxwings.

ELM

Best-suited of the elms for nesting purposes—all of which have buds, blossoms and winged nutlets attractive to birds as food—is the vase-shaped American elm. Its drooping branches provide ideal nesting sites for the hanging nest of the Baltimore oriole, while other birds build in its forked branches. Its great height (up to 120 feet) is attractive to warblers, vireos and wood pewees, as are its many insect inhabitants. Unfortunately, elms are quite susceptible to insect and virus damage. Although this is detrimental to the tree and its appearance, brown creepers, chickadees and woodpeckers find damaged trees valuable. Often-used woodpecker holes become homesites for nuthatches, starlings and hollow-dwelling sparrows.

31

FLOWERING CRAB APPLE

This small-fruited apple has many good features. It has a pleasant shape, offers shade, and has attractive blossoms as well as edible fruits, both for man and bird, thus being an excellent tree for a garden area. Several of the birds which find it desirable for nesting are the robin, cardinal, mockingbird, goldfinch, purple finch and flycatcher. Its fruits, which persist long into the winter, are excellent winter food for such birds as finches, grosbeaks, mockingbirds and crossbills.

FORSYTHIA

The golden bell variety which has a strong growth but rather meager foliage will only be useful for nesting birds if grown against a wall or trellis work, or in a mixed hedge where it will attract catbirds, song and chipping sparrows, mockingbirds, thrashers, cardinals, yellow warblers and wood thrushes.

FUCHSIA

In those parts of the country where the winter is mild, the fuchsia can be grown into a fair-sized bush or made into a very neat hedge by annual clipping. Smaller birds such as some warblers and sparrows may nest in it.

GREENBRIER

Not especially useful for landscape purposes, the greenbrier forms dense thickets which are sought for nesting by cardinals, catbirds, thrashers and chipping sparrows. Since its fruits are attractive to nearly fifty species of birds, including waxwings, grosbeaks, finches and bluebirds, this is a good plant to allow to grow over brushpiles or stumps in a "wild" portion of your garden.

HAWTHORN

Of all the trees found in the United States, hawthorn is by far the most popular with all types of birds for nesting purposes. From a bird's point of view it has just the right branch structure if allowed to grow freely, and the leaf coverage is quite adequate. Its thorns are its chief asset and give excellent protection against the larger ground predators. Unfortunately, it is not widely used for hedging, even though its strong, thorny growth makes it ideal for this purpose.

Hawthorn hedges are often clipped year after year to exactly the same height, with the result that the hedge becomes so thick and woody that it is of no use at all to birds. Such a hedge should be allowed to grow freely for a year and then clipped in the autumn, leaving about 6 inches of new growth. It must be allowed to reach a height of about 6 feet and it will then be an exceedingly popular nesting site for blackbirds, thrushes, song and chipping sparrows, cardinals, catbirds, mockingbirds, thrashers and warblers such as yellowthroats or yellow-breasted chats.

Hawthorn growing freely as a standard tree will look very attractive in the spring with its white blossoms. Its autumn berries are a useful source of food for robins, finches, thrushes, grouse, bobwhites, grosbeaks. It is used for nesting by robins and thrushes, mourning doves, goldfinches, and even magpies.

Strange though it may seem, road hedges are very popular nesting sites. This is partly because so many hedges consist mainly of hawthorn, but it may also be due to the fact that birds find there are fewer predators near the roadway. The headlights of cars at night will keep away many of the nesting birds' nocturnal enemies and the traffic during the day will act as a deterrent to daylight robbers.

HAZELNUT

A free-growing hazelnut tree is of little value to garden birds, with the exception of the mourning dove. Even if grown as a hedge it does not make a particularly good nesting site. Hazelnuts will, of course, be appreciated by woodpeckers, nuthatches, bluejays, grosbeaks, thrashers.

HOLLY

There are quite a number of different kinds of holly; some of these are extremely prickly, while others are not. The prickly type has a very tough twig texture. If grown as a closely-clipped hedge it is almost impossible for a bird to get in and out and equally impossible for it to move around inside, and a hedge of this sort will harbor very few nests. But if free-growing, early-nesters such as mourning doves and English sparrows will use it for nesting. Its leaves, fallen on the ground help to deter cats and other predators.

The non-prickly kinds, if free-growing, tend to have rather drooping branches, but with judicious cutting back they can be made thicker. Thrashers, mourning doves, cardinals and catbirds are likely to use such trees and shrubs.

Hollies, though slow growing, are well worth a place in the garden, the variegated types being especially attractive. From the birds' point of view they afford protection from the weather all the year round and in winter their berries are a great standby.

HONEYSUCKLE

There are several forms of this, and it is better to select one which makes a vigorous growth. In order to keep it bushy it must be vigorously pruned each year, the long, new shoots being cut back by about half their length.

It may be trained on a wall trellis or, better still, over a rustic arch about 7 feet in height, after wire netting of 1 inch mesh has been put across the tope of the arch. A good place to train honeysuckle is round the stump of an old tree, thus converting what may be an eyesore into something pleasant to look at. Evergreen honeysuckle grown against a house wall makes a good roosting place and provides nest sites for smaller garden birds such as sparrows and warblers. If the honeysuckle is thick and nest support is strong, many larger garden birds will use it for nesting, but it is especially valuable for its fruits. Hummers find its blossoms inviting.

HORNBEAM

These are usually seen as free-growing trees and are of little value to birds as such. Hornbeam is sometimes grown as a hedge mixed with ordinary beech, copper beech and yew, which provides a very pleasing variation of color. Such a hedge, if 6 feet high and 2 feet thick, will make an attractive nesting place for large and small garden birds. It takes well to pruning and withered leaves hanging on all winter provide good cover. Its seeds are eaten by a number of birds.

IVY

The common ivy seen on old houses and outbuildings has always had rather a bad name for destroying mortar and making a house damp. It is quite true that it does destroy the mortar because it feeds on it, but it will only make a wall damp if the foliage is thin and the

34

rain can penetrate to the wall. If ivy is very thick, it keeps the wall dry and well protected from the weather. The natural slope of its leaves acts like a thatch. There is some truth in the old saying "the ivy keeps the wall up," for if the ivy is removed the outer skin of the brickwork is removed with it, thereby exposing it to the rain and frost which will cause rapid crumbling.

The main value of wall ivy is that it affords such magnificent protection from rain, wind, snow and frost and therefore provides first-class roosting quarters for all garden birds, which are quite safe from predators if the ivy is grown to a height of 6 feet or more; but it is not to be recommended except on a high garden wall or an unwanted outbuilding.

English sparrows, starlings, blackbirds, robins, flycatchers, wrens and grackles are all fond of wall ivy as a nesting site.

LARCH

The larch is a deciduous conifer, growing best in lime soils. Its branches are pendulous or horizontal, and it is therefore not much use to garden birds for nesting. The seeds of the large cones attract siskins, finches, nuthatches, redpolls and crossbills.

LILAC

Since pruning a lilac eliminates its blossoms for a year, most people allow it to grow freely. In this state, its foliage and branch structure are too sparse to be of any value to nesting birds except for goldfinches and other small birds. If, however, it is cut back for some reason, it will make strong growth and there will then be nesting possibilities for birds such as thrushes, vireos and catbirds. A way of having both blooms and thicker growth is to cut back a third of the shrub each year for a three-year period.

The drawing shows how a lilac which has been allowed to grow too big has been cut back with a saw. The cut surface has been made horizontal as a future foundation for the nests of mourning doves or robins. Both these birds are fond of lilac for their early nests in April when there is very little leaf cover available. Below the cut surface, new shoots will spring out in the following year, giving excellent concealment for nests of other birds. The many insects attracted to fragrant early spring blossoms are excellent food for early hatching nestlings.

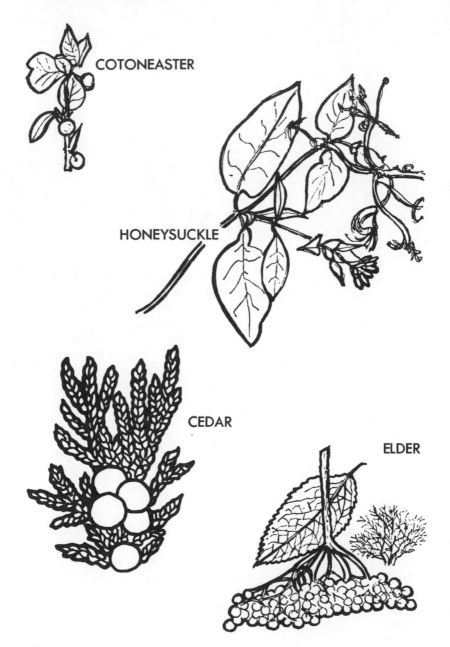

COTONEASTER

HONEYSUCKLE

CEDAR

ELDER

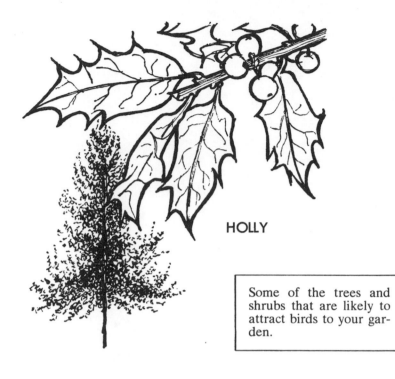

HOLLY

Some of the trees and shrubs that are likely to attract birds to your garden.

BOX

HAWTHORN

37

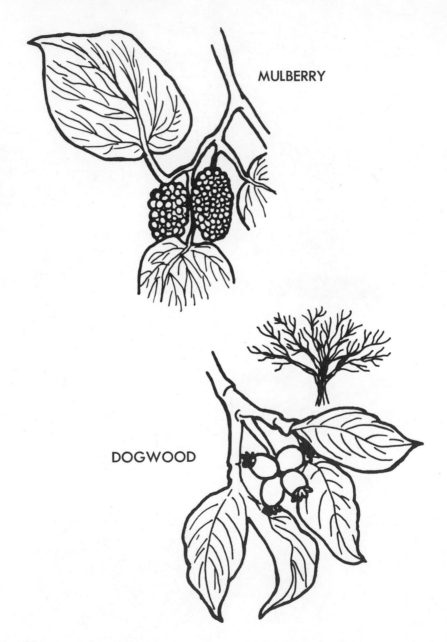

MULBERRY

DOGWOOD

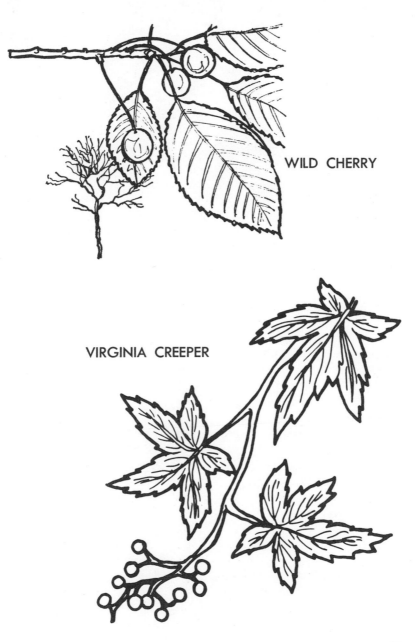

WILD CHERRY

VIRGINIA CREEPER

MAPLE

Most varieties of maple are large trees with an open type of branch structure which is quite unsuitable for nesting garden birds although blue jays, robins, warbling vireos and the ruby-throated hummingbird may find suitable sites. The small ornamental trees also have the wrong type of branch structure making them more important as a food source than for nesting purposes. The Ash-leaved maple, or box elder, is particularly attractive to Evening grosbeaks and purple finches.

MOUNTAIN ASH

Not really a true ash, the mountain ash is actually related to the apple and pear. Although its foliage provides only fair nesting cover, its attractive shape and scarlet fruits relished by robins, waxwings, grosbeaks, thrashers, orioles and red-headed woodpeckers, make it a worthwhile garden tree.

MULBERRY

This tree, in fruit, is attractive to nearly all songbirds. Its soft, juicy fruits ripen in early summer making excellent food for nestlings. Since fruits drop freely and may stain easily, do not plant near sidewalks, patios or clotheslines! This tree offers good cover and nest sites for many species of birds. It is one of the best all-round trees and should be included in every bird garden.

OAKS

These large-growing trees are used primarily in gardens as shade trees. While young oaks offer nest sites to thrushes, robins, vireos and doves, the larger trees are utilized by jays, pewees, tanagers, hawks and woodpeckers. Insects are attracted to the trees which then attract insect-eating birds. Acorns attract larger seed-eaters as well as squirrels.

OLIVE (AUTUMN AND RUSSIAN)

These trees and shrubs have rather recently become popular with bird gardeners. They have silvery-green foliage and are excellent for mass plantings or hedging. Their colorful berries are among the best winter bird feeds, attracting more than thirty species. Nest sites are provided for many of the hedge-dwelling species.

POPLAR

All types of poplar, including Lombardy, are useless as nesting sites for garden birds, their foliage being too thin and their fork structure unsuitable to support all but the tiny hanging nests of birds such as the warbling vireo.

PRIVET

It is most unfortunate for garden birds that privet enjoys such wide popularity. From a gardener's point of view it makes the ideal hedge, but from a bird's point of view the neat, well-clipped privet hedge is the last place in the world for a nesting site. The twig structure is too dense for a bird to enter and the height from the ground is usually insufficient.

The only possible way to make such a privet hedge at all useful for nesting birds is to allow it to grow about 6 inches a year until it is 6 feet high, and to trim out the inside of the hedge periodically. The appearance of the hedge will certainly not be so neat, but such birds as chipping sparrows, robins, thrushes and some warblers may then use it for nesting.

PYRACANTHA (FIRETHORN)

These decorative shrubs, if free-growing, do not have a branch structure of much use to nesting birds, but grown up against walls or trellis work and kept fairly well-clipped to promote thicker growth, it makes an excellent site for the nests of catbirds, thrashers, cardinals, thrushes, and is a good place to put an open-fronted box for a robin. Pyracantha has a strong twig texture with some very sharp projections which act as a deterrent to climbing cats. It can also be grown free as a "standard" up to 9 feet high, and will look very imposing if kept lightly pruned to preserve its shape. Its dark green leaves and bright orange berries make the firethorn an attractive addition to any garden as well as providing winter food.

Close relatives, known as cotoneaster, may be selected for planting as low-growing ground shrubs in rock gardens or upon embankments. These are not very suitable for nesting, except by low-nesting sparrows and warblers, but their red fruits are excellent winter food.

RHODODENDRON

Beloved by gardeners, the evergreen rhododendrons and their

41

smaller-leaved relatives, azaleas, are of little value to birds for nesting purposes or food. They do, however, provide winter cover and some of the ground-nesting birds such as fox, song and white-throated sparrows, yellowthroats and towhees may find protection beneath their broad leaves. Of course the varied flowers add much color to a spring garden.

ROSE (CLIMBING)

A climbing rose must be grown on trellis work, over an archway, or against the stump of a dead tree, if it is to attract nesting birds. The older and thicker the rose, the better. The chief disadvantage with roses is that the old and strong wood, which is what the bird needs most for nest foundation, must be pruned out if the rose is to look its best. Catbirds, thrashers, mockingbirds, sparrows and even warblers may nest in the protection of its thorns.

ROSE (MULTIFLORA)

This provides excellent protection and cover both for nesting and non-nesting birds. It is especially useful as a live fence as its thorny tangle repels predators and its abundant fruits make it attractive to wintering robins, cedar waxwings and bluebirds. White-throated, chipping and field sparrows, chats, juncos, catbirds, cardinals, thrashers and mockingbirds find it useful both for food and nesting.

SNOWBERRY

This graceful shrub has too flimsy a twig texture to be of any real use to nesting birds unless it is grown in thick clumps and occasionally clipped. Song and chipping sparrows might then nest in it. It is, however, an extremely valuable winter food source for both game birds and song birds such as thrushes, cardinals, towhees, grosbeaks and waxwings.

SPIRAEA

This group of shrubs offers a wide range of form and color which makes them popular garden ornamentals. Probably the most common garden shrub is the arching bridal wreath. This shrub, because of its slender twigs, is not very suitable for nest sites except for a few of the smaller birds such as yellow or chestnut-sided warbler, flycatchers and the song and chipping sparrows. Other, sturdier species may offer nest sites to a robin, vireo or cardinal. Spiraea should be included in a mixed shrub border as their blossoms attract many insects.

SYCAMORE

From a garden bird's point of view this tree when free-growing is almost useless as it does not provide the right sort of branch structure at a suitable height. Apart from the millions of insects which it often attracts, it has little advantage to birds. It is, however, used extensively in city areas as a shade tree as it is particularly tolerant of pollution. The mottled trunk may be used to support nest boxes.

VIBURNUM

This large shrub family includes many species which are of value to birds. They grow easily, are ornamental, and most have attractive flowers and fruits relished by songbirds. The majority are well-suited for shrub borders wherein they provide many homesites. Some, such as the blackhaw, are good specimen shrubs and, having dense foliage offer nesting sites to any of the shrub-nesters. Nannyberry forms thickets which are attractive to catbirds, hermit thrushes, chats, rose-breasted grosbeaks and mockingbirds. The maple-leaved viburnum is a smaller shrub form which provides good cover for ground-nesters such as the towhee.

All of these, and other varieties, are especially good food sources for fall migrants such as bluebirds, phoebes, thrushes, robins, catbirds, thrashers, grosbeaks, cedar waxwings, game birds, flickers and pileated woodpeckers as well. Several of these shrubs should be included in any planting for the birds.

VIRGINIA CREEPER

One might think that Virginia creeper would be ideal for birds but, except in very old vines, there is no solid structure on which a bird can fix a nest. Virginia creeper grows flat against the wall, relying on its suckers to keep it up. If grown on a trellis, fence, or dead tree, it then provides a well-protected nesting site for sparrows, thrushes, robins, catbirds, vireos, flycatchers, finches and the rose-breasted grosbeak.

43

Its blue berries, contrasting with scarlet foliage in the fall, are ripe at a time when most insects have died or gone into hibernation, thus making this a valuable food supply for the previously mentioned birds plus flickers, woodpeckers, scarlet tanagers and orioles as well.

WEEDS AND GRASSES

A piece of rough ground covered by long grass, with thistles, groundsel, shepherd's purse, chickweed, dandelions and other weeds, with here and there some brushwood to act as nest support, is of considerable value to garden birds. Those which nest on or near the ground, such as the warbler family, frequently choose an area like this in which to nest. A yellow-breasted chat, for example, may build its nest on old brushwood within a clump of thistles, the latter acting as a deterrent to many predators. Towhees, several of the warblers and sparrows like nesting in weedy patches under a tuft of dead grass.

Many garden birds use long pieces of dead grass for nest construction and often have difficulty finding it in built-up areas where gardens are kept highly cultivated.

Seeding weeds form an important part of the diet of finches. Insectivorous birds will generally find much more insect life in a rough part of a garden than in a more cultivated part.

Where space allows, therefore, a piece of "wild" garden is a great asset to the local bird population.

WEEPING WILLOW, BEECH, BIRCH, CHERRY

It is very unfortunate that all the attractive varieties of "weeping" trees are quite useless for nesting birds except for orioles and ruby-throated hummingbirds as the branch structure is unsuitable.

WILLOW

Free-growing willow trees of all varieties are of little value to nesting birds, but the pollarded willows sometimes seen beside rivers develop, as a result of constant cutting back, a thick stumpy growth with numerous holes and crannies. Such a tree can provide many nesting sites for a variety of birds including owls, wood ducks, brown creepers, flycatchers, titmice and nuthatches as well as the more common garden birds.

WISTERIA

Wisteria, beautiful though it is when in full bloom, is not of great value to nesting birds. It is a slow growing vine which can be a nuisance if it gets round drainpipes or gutters. Sparrows are particularly fond of the flowering shoots. A very old wisteria which is thick and twisted may be used by cardinals, thrushes, English sparrows, robins, thrashers and flycatchers for nesting.

YEW

Many varieties of yew are commonly used in landscaping. Like the boxwood, yew may be used in the old topiary style of landscape gardening and can be, by patient clipping and trimming, fashioned into neat hedges and interesting shapes. Grown in this way, yew is far too thick for most nesting birds. Yew hedges are attractive and make good windbreaks. Though they are by no means the ideal hedge from a bird's point of view, they can be fairly useful if kept lightly clipped and allowed to grow only a few inches a year until about 6 feet high. Grown in this way, yellow warblers, finches and sparrows will nest.

A free-growing yew can be made attractive to nesting birds by cutting back all long, straggly branches to keep the tree in a bushy shape. If the leading end of a long yew branch is cut off, a thick bushy growth will sprout from the sides of the branch. Sparrows are particularly fond of such a nesting site.

Another method of obtaining nesting sites, which applies particularly to the free-growing yew because of its long straight branches, is to pull the branches together in the form of a column, by encircling them with twine. The growing ends of the branches should be cut off to increase side sprouting. After about two years this will develop a very thick tree affording good nesting sites for robins, catbirds, thrushes and mourning doves.

CONCLUSION

As a general rule large trees such as the oak, sycamore, beech, maple, elm and ash are of very little use to garden birds for nesting purposes, for the simple reason that they do not provide the right sort of nesting site at the correct height, with the necessary leaf-cover and twig structure. Larger birds like crows, bluejays, and the common grackle will use such trees, but these species seem well able to look after themselves and so do not need encouragement. Big trees, however, particularly oaks, maples and sycamores, do provide a valuable source of insect life, which is much sought after by smaller birds such as warblers, titmice, creepers, nuthatches and chickadees.

In a small garden large trees can be a problem. In the spring and summer they take up a great deal of moisture with their spreading roots. Their shade is welcome sometimes on a hot day, but they deprive many surrounding shrubs and flowers of sunlight and stunt their growth. In the autumn the leaves and seedlings of big trees can be a nuisance, while in the winter, snow may break boughs off, creating quite a lot of trouble.

One solution which may suit both man and the garden birds is to pollard the tree, provided it is not too large. The growth of the tree is then under control and the sprouting branches can be pruned back every year or two. It will look quite neat when the leaves are on it and will be much more useful to nesting garden birds.

As we have seen, it is the trees of medium and small size which are most useful to birds. Some of these are evergreen and others deciduous, and by correct pruning and cutting these can be made into ideal nesting sites.

If garden birds had a choice of nesting place from among all the trees listed above, the tree-nesting birds would almost certainly choose the hawthorn. This is certainly the best deciduous tree, while the best evergreens are probably the pines and hemlocks, which provide weather protection throughout the year and are thus very useful for roosting and nesting. These are particularly ideal for mourning doves and robins, which often start nesting operations at the end of March when leaf cover is very difficult to find. The American holly comes a close second, but its usefulness is limited by the fact that it grows only in areas with rather mild winters.

Wild blackberry, multiflora rose, mulberries, viburnums, and dogwoods all come high on the list. Of the climbing plants wall ivy is perhaps the best all-rounder, while honeysuckle and Virginia creeper are particularly good as they grow rapidly and provide good food supplies as well. Pyracantha and greenbrier have spiny projections offering well-protected nest sites especially if supported on trellises or fencing.

46

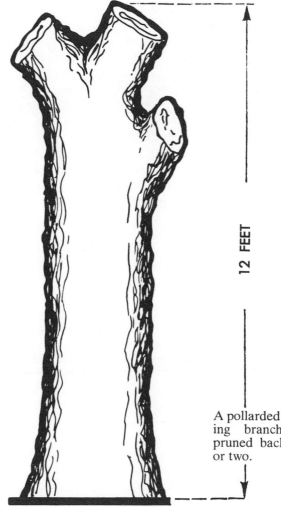

12 FEET

A pollarded tree. Sprouting branches can be pruned back every year or two.

ONE METHOD OF PLANTING A GARDEN TO ATTRACT GARDEN BIRDS

This garden is designed for smaller suburban lots of ¼ acre or less. To make maintenance practical on larger properties, more space should be allowed to develop naturally.

1. Multiflora rose hedge or cultivated blackberry. 2. Pruned fruit trees (apple, cherry, crab apple, pear). 3. Brush pile and patch of natural grasses and weeds. 4. Mixed shrub border including any of the following: viburnums, lilacs, mulberries, forsythia, highbush blueberry, elderberry, inkberry, blackhaw, black alder, red-twig dogwood, weigela, mockorange, spicebush, autumn olive, andromeda, nannyberry, honeysuckle, pyracantha, barberry, privet, chokecherry, euonymus, deutzia, spiraea or buddleia. Including several evergreens will provide not only nesting sites, and food, but cover during the winter when other shrubs have lost their leaves. 5. Trellis with climbing rose, honeysuckle, clematis, Virginia creeper, bittersweet or grape. 6. Shallow rock-edged pool surrounded by rock garden plants. If space is limited, any bird bath could be substituted here. 7. Small flowering trees: dogwood, mountain ash, crab apple, hawthorn, hackberry, mulberry, cornelian cherry. 8. Clump of birches, mulberries, chokecherries or sour gum. 9. Annuals or perennial flowers around patio. Additional flower borders and roses may be placed in front of shrubbery or around house as desired. 10. House with front foundation planting of evergreen shrubs: yews, hollies, cedars, juniper or pine. Popular azaleas and rhododendrons, though not especially attractive to birds, add color and interest to foundation or evergreen plantings. 11. Garage with trellises for climbing vines. Use any listed under 5 or pyracantha, matrimony vine, ivy. 12. Evergreens such as holly, juniper, white pine, hemlock or red cedar may be used to provide neat, attractive boundaries along front sides of one's property. These have some value as nest sites and for food, but their greatest value is for roosting and as cover in winter. 13. Low rock wall or fence with climbing roses or vines. This could also be a flower bed.

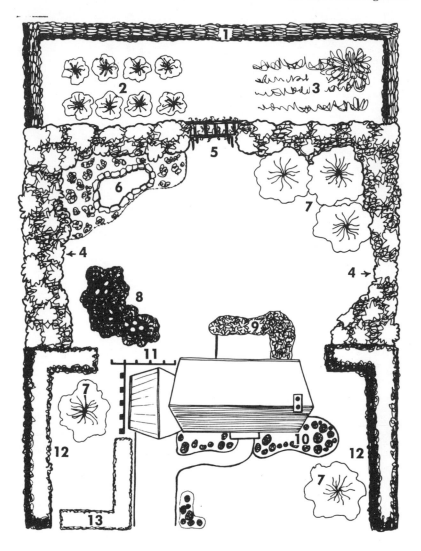

CHAPTER THREE

Artificial Nesting Sites

WHEREVER THERE IS a shortage of natural nesting sites we must try to provide an alternative. This can be done for quite a number of birds if we know what is required.

Some tree-nesting birds, particularly the robin, have already adapted themselves to building in open nest boxes, in garden sheds, on drainpipes and in many odd places in close proximity to man. This shows a trend in bird behavior of which we must take full advantage.

Generally speaking, a nesting site against the wall of a house can be made one of the safest places for a bird to rear her young. The presence of man automatically helps to keep away a lot of the nesting bird's greatest enemies, and if the artificial nesting device is correctly placed the risk from cats, rats and mice can be reduced to a minimum. The house wall is one of the best places in any garden on which to fix nesting devices, and moreover it may be the only place available in some of the newer housing developments where large dividing hedges, fences or walls are not allowed.

NEST BOXES FOR WRENS, CHICKADEES,
NUTHATCHES, TITMICE AND DOWNY WOODPECKERS

1. Construction

Nesting boxes can be made in many different ways. They can be

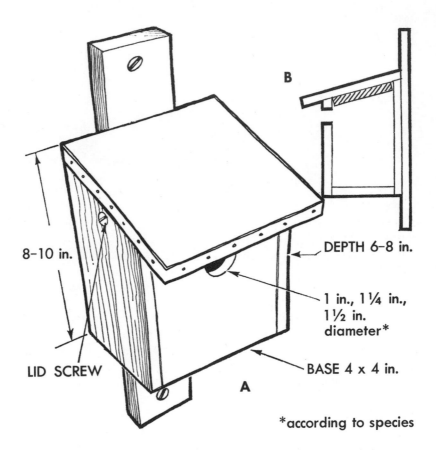

B

8-10 in.

DEPTH 6-8 in.

1 in., 1 ¼ in.,
1 ½ in.
diameter*

LID SCREW

A

BASE 4 x 4 in.

*according to species

Nest box for wrens, chickadees, nuthatches, titmice and downy woodpeckers. A Front view. B Cross-section showing roof reinforcement.

cut out of an old log, they can be made of the most expensive wood and finely finished or they can be put together in an amateurish way with old bits of wood. All will be used by birds provided the conditions given below are fulfilled.

The construction should be on the same lines as shown in **A** at left, using wood not less than ¾ inch thick. The size of the entrance hole is most important. It must not be more than 1-1¼ inches in diameter for house wrens and Bewick's wrens, 1¼" for nuthatches, chickadees, titmice, 1½" for Carolina wrens. The entrance hole should be placed about ¾ of an inch from the top and need not be central. A perch under the hole is not required, in fact it is a disadvantage because it gives sparrows an opportunity to sit on the perch and annoy the occupant. Wrens are so acrobatic that they have no difficulty at all in flying straight up to the nesting hole and clinging to the sides of it before entering. The roof of the wren box should overhang the entrance hole by about 2 inches. This overhang keeps out the weather and makes it much more difficult for squirrels or cats to attack the occupant from above or for field mice to climb into the box.

The roof of the box must be removable in order to clear out the old nest. For sanitary reasons, wrens do not like breeding on top of an old nest in which there have been young birds. Hinges are generally not satisfactory as the roof may be subject to slight movement in a high wind. The best way to get a snug fitting is to fix a piece of wood on the under-surface of the roof in such a way that it fits into the top of the box, (see shaded part in **B**), thus providing something into which a screw can be fixed on each side. If the screws are oiled before they are put in, they can easily be removed each year for cleaning out the box.

Another advantage of using screws instead of hinges is that it prevents people from having a well-intended peep to see "how things are getting on." Such interference is never appreciated by the bird and she may desert her eggs unless incubation is well under way and the eggs are near to hatching. This rule applies to all garden birds. The less they are disturbed, the better.

Most birds have no sense of smell, so it does not matter if the box smells of creosote or wood preservative. Roofing material should always be put on the roof and any crack which might let in a draft should be sealed.

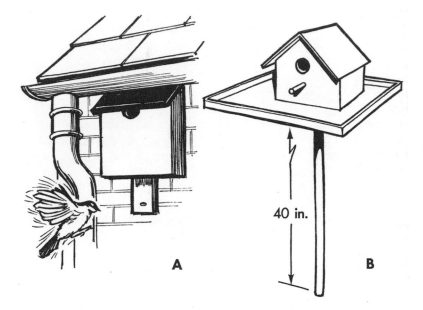

How nest boxes should and should not be placed. **A.** The box
is ideally placed under the eaves of a garage or outbuilding at
the correct height (6 to 10 feet). **B.** A combination tit box and
bird table which has everything wrong with it. The box is too
big and the hole is too big. It has been placed on a feeding
table in an open place at a height (40 in.) which would make

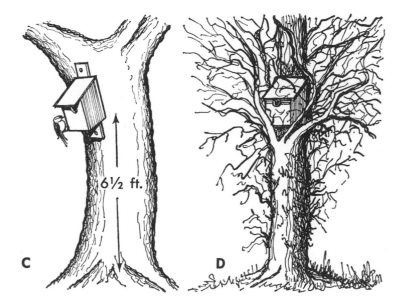

it very easy for a cat to spring up onto the table. **C.** This box has been well placed at the correct height 6½ ft.) on the underslope of a large tree which has smooth bark. **D.** A good wren box, but badly placed. It will be accessible to cats and field mice, and with foliage obstructing the view round the entrance, wrens will ignore the box.

2. Positioning

The position of the box is the next important thing. It must always be placed out of the reach of cats, rats, mice and squirrels. As none of the latter can climb a well-built brick wall, the walls of a house or building are generally the safest place and should be considered first. The box should be placed at a height from 6 to 10 feet; thus, if it is placed close under the eaves of a garage, outbuilding or bungalow it will be in an ideal position, with protection from above and below.

It is hardly necessary to say that the box should be fixed very firmly so that there is no movement in a wind. This is best done by hammering a fixing board to the back of the box before putting it up, which makes nailing to the wall much easier, and also prevents dampness from getting into the back.

If the box is sheltered under the eaves of a roof, it does not matter if it faces north, south, east or west.

When fixing wren boxes on trees, it is always best to choose the trunk of a large tree with smooth bark. An underslope of the trunk, or a large branch coming off the trunk is better still, for this makes it more inaccessible to climbing predators, and the wrens certainly won't worry about their box being tilted at an angle.

Wren boxes on trees should never have any branches near the entrance hole. Wrens like an unobstructed view when entering and leaving their nest, and do not like perches for predators just outside the nest. Weasels and field mice, for example, can more easily gain access to a wren box if branches grow across the entrance hole. This is a very important point—in fact, it is really a waste of time putting up a wren box surrounded by branches.

Boxes on trees should not be placed facing south into the full sun but should face west, or north-west if the position is exposed. There is, however, no hard and fast rule about this, and it depends a great deal on shelter provided by nearby trees.

Generally speaking, remember when fixing wren boxes that there should never be anything between the bottom of the box and the ground, and no foliage in front of it. Once the box has been successfully occupied, don't move it, because it will almost certainly be used every year by the original occupants or their progeny. If the box is not occupied, its site should be changed.

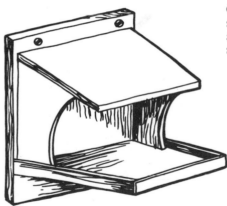

Open-fronted nesting shelf for robins, phoebes and song sparrows; and a shelf for barn swallows.

NESTING SHELVES FOR ROBINS, PHOEBES, BARN SWALLOWS AND SONG SPARROWS

A simple nesting shelf with a roof, open front, and open or partially open sides is suitable for some non-cavity nesting species. Robins and phoebes normally build in trees or shrubs, but will utilize man-made nesting shelves. Barn swallows and song sparrows which usually locate nests on beams beneath overhangs of buildings, will readily accept nest shelves, especially in an area where there is a lack of suitable buildings.

Place nesting shelves 6 to 15 feet off the ground. Excellent places are under awnings, beneath overhangs or eaves of house, garage or garden shed. Other suitable locations are on fences, walls, or vine-covered trellises.

The bottom of the shelf should be a seven inch square with ¾″ or one inch edging. The back should be 6 to 8 inches high with a sloping roof, 8½ inches square. As with bird houses, natural woods or dull colors are preferable and more readily accepted by the birds. Don't forget to drill several ¼ inch holes in the bottom for drainage.

ARTIFICIAL HOLES IN TREES

An artificially-made hole in a dead or partly-dead tree is a useful alternative to a nesting box, and although there is no evidence that such holes are preferred to nest boxes—indeed, it may be the other way round, for some birds will sometimes leave natural holes if boxes are available—it is always interesting to see how different birds react to the different housing offered.

A tree hole should be about 8 to 10 inches deep, 4 inches in width and 6 to 8 inches in height. If the entrance hole is 1⅛ inches in diameter, it will be suitable for chickadees, and, at the same time, be too small for English sparrows. A 1¼ inch-diameter hole is suitable for nuthatches, tufted titmice, house wrens and the downy wood-pecker. After chipping out the hole, the front should be fitted, using wood about ¾ inch thick. It can be secured in position by a vertical strip of wood, as shown, leaving the nails half hammered in so that the front can be removed easily for cleaning purposes. The hole should be about 8 feet from the ground, preferably on the under-slope of a tree to make it more difficult for cats and squirrels to interfere.

Nuthatches may use such a nesting hole, as they will also use ordinary bird boxes. If the hole is too small they can enlarge it, and if too big they will plaster it up with mud to keep out unwelcome visitors. They also plaster up any cracks in the nest box, including the inside of the lid, which is an important point to remember for anyone inspecting the nest box. Strangely enough, although the nuthatch has a very powerful beak, it seems unable to cope with invasion by sparrows.

An open artificial nesting hole can also be very popular with flycatchers. In such a case no fitted front is required but only a piece of wood 1 inch wide, nailed across the bottom of the opening horizontally. Flycatchers need only a shallow nesting site.

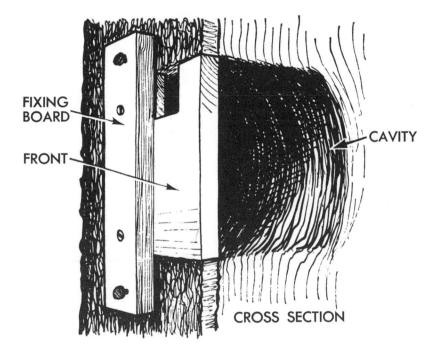

An artificial nesting hole chipped out of a tree.

HOLES IN THE WALLS

A suitable hole in a brick wall is made by removing one brick completely and splitting it lengthways, leaving a thickness of about 1½ inches. Clean out the cavity of loose mortar and then lightly cement the split brick back into place, with a gap about 1 inch at one end of the brick as an opening. The nest cavity can easily be cleaned out each year by tapping out the brick. The nest hole should be not less than 4½ feet from the ground. A piece of slate may be

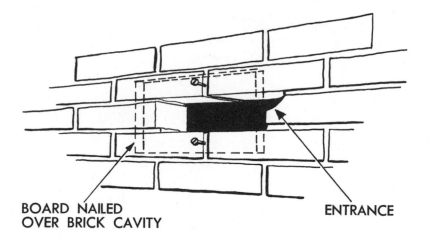

**BOARD NAILED
OVER BRICK CAVITY**   **ENTRANCE**

A nesting site made by a brick cavity in a wall. It should not be less than 4½ feet from the ground.

inserted above the movable front brick as a support for the bricks above. It sounds a tedious process, but it will be very worthwhile and will provide a safe and permanent nesting site for chickadees, swifts and tree swallows.

It is equally effective but less pleasing in appearance to hammer a board over the cavity, chipping a corner off the brick next to the cavity to act as an entrance hole.

Nests in Sheds

To encourage swallows to nest in outbuildings, a small hole about 2 inches x 3 inches wide should be made at the top of a door. The door can then be closed and the swallows can get in and out as they please. A 16-inch length of 2-inch x 2-inch wood should be hammered up on the highest place in the outbuilding in a position where cats, mice or rats cannot climb. It is wise to hang a piece of sacking directly under the nest (like a circus net) as the young swallows will

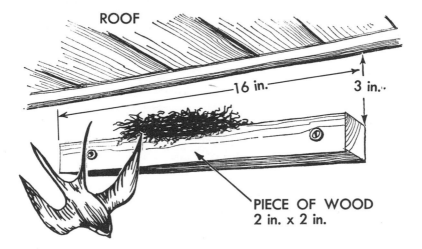

ROOF

16 in. 3 in.

PIECE OF WOOD
2 in. x 2 in.

A nesting site for swallows in an outbuilding.

make a very considerable mess on whatever is below. A similar support can be fixed up in a house porch, provided this does not have a transparent roof, which swallows dislike when nesting.

It is a popular belief that swallows breed under the eaves of houses. This is incorrect. It is the house martin which breeds under eaves. Swallows nearly always build their shallow, cup-shaped nests of mud on some sort of support or ledge such as a cross-beam inside a barn, large shed or garage. The swallow's nest, unlike that of the purple martin, is quite open, so the swallow always likes a good roof over its head to protect the nest from winged predators.

OPEN SHEDS

If there is an "open" shed or a lean-to structure against a wall in the garden, this can always be made into a potential nesting place for sparrows and robins if a shelf is constructed in the highest part beyond the reach of cats, rats and mice.

NESTS ON TRELLIS WORK

The trellis work which we commonly see on houses supporting clematis and other climbing plants is unfortunately of little use to nesting garden birds because it is usually too flimsy and is always fixed too close to the wall. A bird such as a robin cannot find enough nest support on such a trellis unless there happens to be a very thick creeper growing up it.

This lack of nest support can be overcome fairly well on an existing trellis by tying a length of wood 2 inches x 2 inches wide against the trellis at a height of about 6 feet. This will give the necessary support for a nest.

When a new trellis work is made and it is hoped to encourage nesting birds, the trellis should be made in a certain way—it should be square, not diagonal. The horizontal parts should be made of 2-inch x 2-inch lengths of wood, as it is these which provide most of the support for the fairly heavy nest of robins or thrushes. These

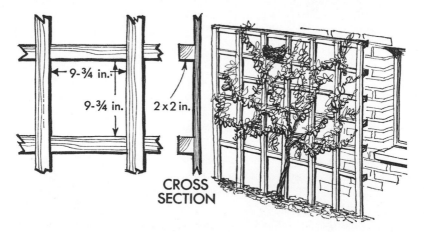

CROSS SECTION

Trellis work suitable for supporting large and small nests

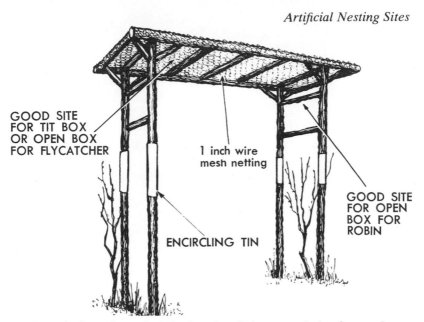

GOOD SITE
FOR TIT BOX
OR OPEN BOX
FOR FLYCATCHER

1 inch wire
mesh netting

GOOD SITE
FOR OPEN
BOX FOR
ROBIN

ENCIRCLING TIN

A typical rustic arch. The bands of tin around the four poles
will prevent cats and squirrels from reaching nest sites.

birds can get nearly all of their nests on a width of 2 inches. The rest
of the nest support is derived from whatever shrub or creeper is
growing up the trellis. The vertical strips need only be 1 inch thick.
The trellis is best fixed to the wall with angle irons.

Trellis work need not necessarily cover a large area, and it is
better if it does not reach to the ground. Six or eight squares of trellis
behind a climbing rose, at a height of 6 to 9 feet, will be good both
for the rose and for nesting birds as well as giving a much neater
appearance to the wall. There are many places on a house where an
ugly wall can be made quite attractive by using trellis work. The
shrubs recommended are honeysuckle, grape, pyracantha, some fruit
trees, forsythia, clematis (but not types that require annual
pruning), bittersweet, Virginia creeper, matrimony vine, climbing
rose and even a domestic blackberry.

NESTS ON ARCHES

A garden always looks better if it contains one or two rustic
arches. Not only do arches "break up" the garden and make it

63

visually more interesting, they also provide a floral display at a higher level and are a great advantage where space is short.

A rustic arch suitable for nesting birds should be about 6 to 9 feet high and measure about 30 inches between horizontal poles. It is a good plan to put 1 inch wire mesh netting over the top of the arch, for this will act as a support for the climbing plant and keep the underside of the arch clear, as well as forming a good foundation for any nest. To increase the leaf cover it is worth growing over the arch something like the clematis montana intermingled with, say, a climbing rose.

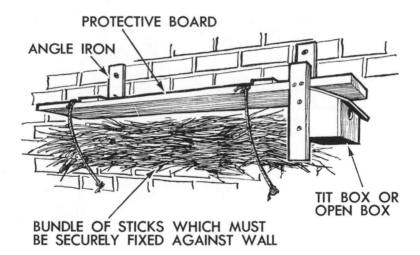

PROTECTIVE BOARD

ANGLE IRON

TIT BOX OR OPEN BOX

BUNDLE OF STICKS WHICH MUST BE SECURELY FIXED AGAINST WALL

Sticks fixed firmly under a protective shelf to attract wrens and thrushes.

BUNDLES OF TWIGS

One method of forming a nesting site which should be particularly attractive to wrens and thrushes is to wire a bundle of sticks together and fix it horizontally at a height of about 6 feet under a protective shelf or under an overhanging roof. It may also be fixed on the wall of a house, but then a protective board must be put above it to hide the nest from above and to keep off rain and sun. Another good place is under a window box on the first floor. In this case a protective board is not necessary.

Bundles of twigs may also be tied vertically to a stake to attract thrushes, robins and wrens. Such bundles are best placed in shrubbery. If there are cats about, it is essential to encircle the sticks with some large mesh wire netting, as shown. The outer edge of the wire netting must be flexible—cats will not risk a jump on to anything that is not firm.

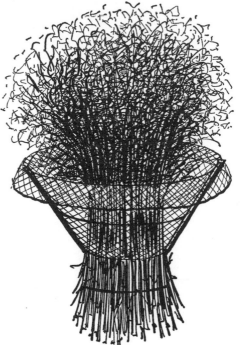

Bundle of twigs to attract thrushes, robins and wrens. Wire netting acts as cat barrier.

ARTIFICIAL SITES FOR BROWN CREEPERS, NUTHATCHES, TITMICE, CHICKADEES, AND DOWNY WOODPECKERS

Brown creepers usually nest behind a fold of bark which protrudes away from the parent tree, or in cracks and crevices in tree

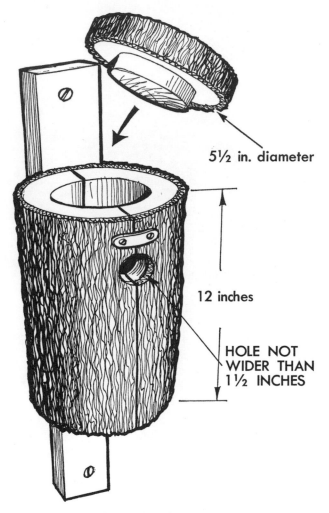

5½ in. diameter

12 inches

HOLE NOT
WIDER THAN
1½ INCHES

A rustic nest box for tree creepers.

trunks. Artificial nesting sites, made of bark, usually attract predators, and nest boxes of the type illustrated are generally safer for the occupants.

A log of wood about 12 inches long and 5½ inches in diameter, with rough bark such as elm or pine, should be cut lengthways down the middle, a slice for the lid having been cut off first. The cavity can then be chiseled out from each half. The depth of the cavity should be about 8 inches and the diameter 4 inches. It is better to carve out what will be the bottom of the cavity rather than replace it afterwards with a different piece of wood. The entrance hole should be oval-shaped and not wider than 1½ inches.

The box must be firmly fixed on the underslope of a tree trunk or large bough, in a fairly secluded place.

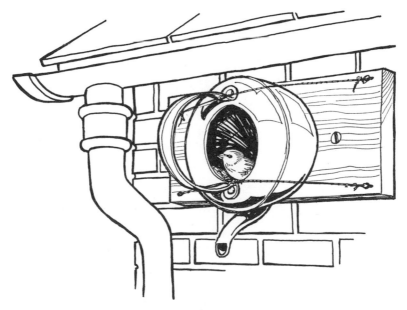

A kettle will make a safe site for a robin's nest.

TEA KETTLES

A tea kettle attached to a board and mounted beneath eaves of a building, as shown in the illustration, may prove to be an interesting

67

and unusual nest site for cavity dwellers. The bowl-shape provides a good nest foundation and protection from the elements, while the spout provides excellent drainage. In addition, the smooth metal surface is a good deterrent of cats, rats and squirrels. However, be sure this nest support is in a shaded place, else the metal become too hot. It will be fascinating to see what kinds of birds will nest in this container.

SPECIAL SITES FOR WRENS

Wrens are particularly fond of sacking as an artificial support for a nest. It is easiest to use a sack, folded so that it is fairly thick, and

Nesting sites for wrens. Sacking can be fixed to the trunk of a tree (**A**) or to the underside of a branch (**B**).

then hammered firmly to the under-side of a leaning tree trunk, or to the under-side of a bough 6 feet from the ground. It can also be fixed under the eaves of a garage or shed.

PURPLE MARTIN HOUSES

Purple martins are sociable birds, preferring to nest in colonies rather than singly. The martin house is a specially designed apartment type structure which allows these birds to congregate. Each compartment is a 6-inch cubicle with a 2½-inch hole near the bottom. A board 20½ inches long by 6 inches high is necessary for the sides to allow for the interior partitions. Eight compartments can be constructed on a tier and two, three or more tiers may be stacked leaving a small air space between them. The center column should be left open for air passage also. Top with a peaked roof with screened air holes and side ventilators.

Two housing arrangements for nesting purple martins: hollowed-out gourds strung from crosspieces, and apartment type structure.

The house should be placed in an open area away from trees and buildings. It should be upon a pole, 15 to 20 feet off the ground. Since martins feed in the air, they need plenty of open space for their swooping flight. Wires located beyond the limits of their approach to their nest boxes will be utilized widely for roosting. Martin houses should be cleaned thoroughly at the end of the nesting season.

A martin house made from gourds can be an interesting addition to a garden. This method of setting up nest sites for purple martins seems to be especially effective in the southern states. The idea supposedly originated with the Indians who were fond of these birds. A tall pole is set up similar to the previous method. A wagon wheel or crossbars are attached at the top. Hollow gourds with entrance holes cut in them are strung from the crosspieces.

Nest Boxes for Barn Owls and Sparrow Hawks

If there is a large tree in the garden, it may be possible to attract barn owls or sparrow hawks by putting up a nesting box made from

Nesting box for owls and sparrow hawks, made like a single-holed dovecote.

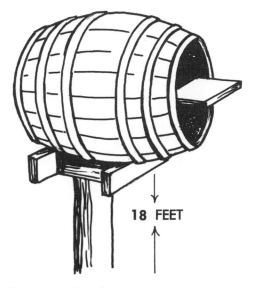

18 FEET

Barrel-type nest box for owls and sparrow hawks.

a wooden barrel. An interior cavity of at least 18 inches by 18 inches is needed. If there is little or no recess for the end pieces, you should remove one end and recess it about 8 inches. If the barrel is too small to allow this, construct a downward sloping awning of wood over the entrance to keep out drafts and rain. A six-inch diameter hole should be cut in the protected end-piece so that its lowest point is about half way down the side of the barrel. A small shelf may be placed below the hole for perching. A four to six inch layer of sawdust or wood chips should be provided inside the barrel as nesting material.

Place the barrel at least 18 feet above the ground on a pole or large tree near an open area or field. Bands of metal flashing 2 feet in width placed above and below the barrel, if mounted upon a tree, will prevent squirrels and raccoons from taking up residency. Although not usually considered garden birds, the owls and hawks should be encouraged to nest in gardens outside of populated areas as they will do much to control small rodents, grasshoppers and other larger insects.

Bluebird Boxes

The bluebird has become a rarity in many areas of the country. This is due to the destruction of former nest sites and the competition for existing cavities with the more aggressive cavity-nesting species such as English sparrows, and starlings.

The simple box, shown in the illustration above, is attractive to bluebirds and is easily constructed. Use soft wood that is ½-inch thick. The bottom should be 5 inches by 5 inches, the sides 5½ inches wide by 9½ inches long against the back, but only 9 inches in length in front. The 7-inch by 7-inch roof should be hinged, or in some other way removable for cleaning. Boxes can be placed on an

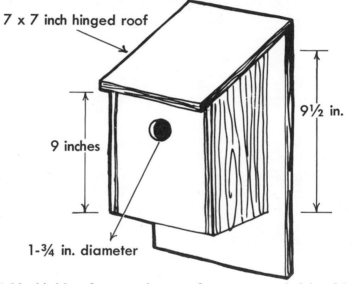

7 x 7 inch hinged roof

9½ in.

9 inches

1-¾ in. diameter

A bluebird box for mounting on a fence post at a height of 3 to 4 feet from the ground.

8-inch by 15-inch backboard for convenient mounting. The entrance hole, 1¾ inches in diameter should be located 1½ inches down from the top.

The placement of your bluebird house is important. A fence post is preferable to a tree trunk and a height of no more than 3 or 4 feet seems to discourage sparrows and starlings. Face the house to the south or southeast overlooking an open field or a roadside area.

NESTING HOLES FOR SWIFTS

These fascinating birds, which spend almost their whole lives on the wing, cannot perch but can only cling to a rough wall long enough to work their way into a nest hole. In old houses, they invariably breed where there are small holes, 1 to 1½ inches in diameter, under the eaves, usually between the fascia board and the top of the house wall. Anyone who has sufficient energy to make a hole of this nature may soon find a swift in occupation. In some areas, swifts are comparatively common birds, but they spend so much time high up in the air that we rarely see them.

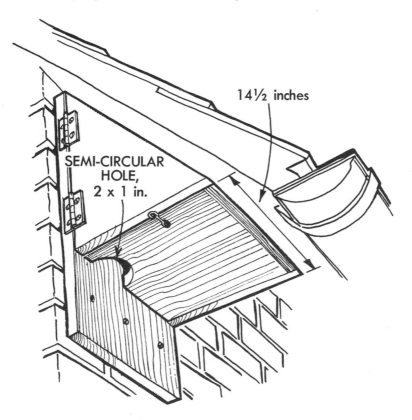

14½ inches

SEMI-CIRCULAR HOLE, 2 x 1 in.

A nesting box for a swift.

The increased use of concrete, glass and metals for new buildings, as opposed to brick and wood, makes it likely that swifts are going to have increasing difficulty in finding nesting holes. Nest boxes have been used and they should be fixed under the eaves, as is shown in the illustration. The important features of the box, which must be made to fit snugly under the eaves, are that it must be about 14½ inches long and the entrance hole must be either underneath or at the side. The entrance hole should measure approximately 2 inches by 1 inch. A small coil of straw placed at the end of the box will provide an artificial nest cup.

PROTECTION OF NESTS FROM PREDATORS

Whenever there is a possibility of any type of nest box or nest in a tree being attacked by cats, squirrels, mice, rats, or weasels it may be a good plan to encircle the tree with a collar of wire netting of the smallest possible mesh. This is not an easy job on a big tree, and it needs quite a lot of wire netting, but it is well worthwhile. Smaller trees which have or are likely to have nests in them should also be wired.

It is not necessary to hammer nails into the tree. The inner part of the wire netting can be held to the trunk by an encircling strand of wire, while the outer edge can be held up by wire or string attached to the branches above. Nothing except perhaps a field mouse can pass such a barrier.

In order to prevent cats climbing an arch, it is a good idea to hammer a length of tin around each of the upright poles. Such a sleeve of tin or other smooth-surfaced material can be utilized in place of the aforementioned wire mesh collar on tree trunks and poles which support nesting boxes and feeders. A measure of this sort is only effective provided there are no adjacent branches or structures from which predators may leap, by-passing the barrier.

A more natural barrier can be developed by underplanting suitable nesting trees with spiny or thorny shrubs such as a multiflora rose, barberry, blackberry, greenbrier, holly or pyracantha. Even cuttings from thorny plants, piled at the base of nesting trees, may prove to be effective barriers. In addition to avoiding an unnatural or cluttered look about the garden, these living plant barriers provide fruits and berries as an added bonus attraction for the birds . . . or the gardener.

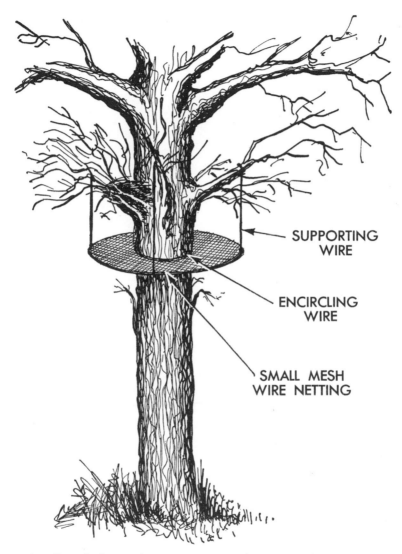

SUPPORTING
WIRE

ENCIRCLING
WIRE

SMALL MESH
WIRE NETTING

A collar of wire netting protects nests from ground predators.

CHAPTER FOUR

Nesting Preferences of Various Birds

IN A GARDEN the choice of trees and shrubs is usually made to suit the needs of man rather than those of birds, thereby limiting the selection of nesting sites from which a bird can choose. A fuller description, therefore, is given below of the types of nesting site a garden bird would select if allowed a freer choice. It relates to what has already been mentioned under the list of trees and shrubs, and is intended to provide an easier method of reference.

BLUEBIRD

Although in the same family as robins and thrushes, the bluebird has different nesting habits. It is a cavity-dweller preferring old apple trees and can best be attracted to nest in a yard by a bluebird box placed in a suitable location. If your garden is in a very built-up area, don't expect to attract any bluebirds as they prefer a farm or orchard setting. In a more rural location, a nice lawn, a birdbath or the following shrubs may help to attract them: bayberry, cotoneaster, mulberry, pyracantha, sumac or viburnums.

BLUE JAY

One of the noisiest of all birds, the blue jay adds color and interest to your garden. It is attracted by cedars, hemlocks, maples, large oaks, pines and good-sized shrubs wherein it locates its nest in a crotch anywhere from 6 to 15 feet up. Though often thought of as a pest, and bully, if food is plentiful, blue jays are not bossy, and in fact, are excellent sentinels of the garden. They can be kept away from smaller songbird feeders by provision of a separate feeder area with peanuts, sunflower seeds, bread and suet.

BOBWHITE

Although a game bird rather than a song bird, the bobwhite may visit your garden if your property is near a field or woodland edge where it normally dwells. If sufficient food, especially lespedeza, abounds, it may nest also. Nests are on the ground, in clumps of dried grasses or tangled vegetation.

BROWN CREEPER

This bird builds in vertical crevices such as those found when loose bark splits away from a tree trunk. Also, it might nest behind a loose board in a barn or shed. It will breed in nest boxes.

BROWN THRASHER

The thrasher may nest on the ground, in thickets, or low in thorny bushes and shrubs. It can be attracted to your garden by plantings of barberry, blackberry, grape, greenbrier, hawthorn, honeysuckle, matrimony vine, multiflora rose and viburnums. In addition to the fruits of these plants, the fruits of bayberry, black cherry, cornelian cherry, dogwood, holly, huckleberry, inkberry and mulberry are relished. Feeder foods include raisins, grapes, berries, suet, nutmeats and small bits of cheese.

CARDINALS

Dense shrubbery, small trees, hedges and briars offer likely nest sites for the popular cardinal, one of the easiest of the birds to attract to your garden and feeder. Plants specifically used for nesting include the barberry, blackberry, cherry, crab apple, forsythia, grape, greenbrier, lilac, multiflora rose, spiraea, viburnums. Though primarily seed-eaters, harmful insects are also taken. Winter feeder foods include sunflower seeds, nutmeats, cracked corn, mixed seeds and bread.

CATBIRD

The catbird prefers to nest in tangles of shrubs with vines growing over them. Nesting of these gray birds with their mewing call may be encouraged by the same plantings which attract the brown thrasher, as well as by lilac or mock orange. Food preferences are the same as well, although the thrasher will eat a bit more insect matter than the catbird does.

CHICKADEES

These cavity nesters are easily attracted to both nest boxes and feeders. They particularly like old apple and birch trees which not only supply nesting sites but a plentiful supply of insect food as well. If you do not have some of these old trees, it is certainly worthwhile to erect some nest boxes for these inquisitive, acrobatic creatures who will become year-round residents.

ENGLISH SPARROW

The English sparrow nests in holes in any type of building, in drainpipes, ventilators, purple martin nests, tree holes, wall ivy, windowsill ledges beneath air conditioners, and in nest boxes. It will build its own nest, if necessary, high up in any garden tree. Prolific to the point of being pests in some areas, these finches introduced from England readily eat bread strewn on the ground and may thus be kept from feeders.

FINCHES

The purple finch usually nests in evergreens such as white pine and spruce, orchard trees or deciduous shrubs only in the far northern United States or parts of Canada. During the winter months, however, they may visit gardens in almost any state. Nearly any seed, but especially sunflower seeds, will attract them to your feeders.

Originally native only to western states, the similar house finch was introduced in the East and seems to be thriving in the greater metropolitan New York area. Here it nests in gardens, favoring ornamental evergreens and shrubs near buildings although it will also reside in nest boxes, while in its natural range it frequents sagebrush, mountain mahogany, saltbush and cactus as well as varied trees. They eat weed seeds, mulberries and cherries.

FLYCATCHERS

The many species of flycatchers have varied nesting habits most of which can be encouraged in the home garden. Crested flycatchers nest in tree or post cavities, bird boxes, and even mailboxes while phoebes nest in crevices, under eaves or porches, in garden sheds, or on nesting shelves. The smaller flycatchers and wood pewees may partially suspend nests on twig forks, 4 to 20 feet high, build in low shrubs, or build in a shade tree anywhere from 8 to 40 feet in height. Thus there is a wide range of plants which will attract them, from andromeda or spiraea, to crab apples, dogwoods or even large oaks.

GOLDFINCH

The goldfinch, dependent upon weed and flower seeds, is a late-nester. It can often be attracted to suburban gardens where it will nest in shrubs, brier patches, and a variety of trees, particularly if the garden contains a weedy patch with asters, burdock, catnip, chickory, dandelions, evening primrose, goldenrod, mullein, sunflower and thistle. The fruits of alder, birch, elm, sycamore and conifers are also attractive food sources.

GRACKLES

The common grackle nests in colonies, usually in evergreens near water. Boat-tailed grackles frequent coastal marshes and inland streams of the southern states. They will nest in cat-tails, high grasses or tall willows. Although their food is mostly animal matter, migrating flocks may damage grain crops. Wintering birds will accept almost any food—bread, seed, suet or berries, and it is at this time that they are most likely to visit your garden.

GROSBEAKS

Rose-breasted (Eastern) and black-headed (Western) grosbeaks may nest in any deciduous tree in your garden. Primarily seed and bud eaters, these birds may be encouraged to remain year-round by a good supply of sunflower seeds. Such seeds may also attract migrant evening grosbeaks during the winter. These flocking birds will nest in conifers while the southern blue grosbeak can be attracted to nest in hedge borders. Apple, barberry, birches, cherry, cone-bearing trees and shrubs, dogwood, hawthorn, lilac, locust, maple, mountain ash, sumac, tulip trees and Virginia creeper all provide natural winter foods attractive to grosbeaks.

HUMMINGBIRDS

The ruby-throated hummingbird builds a tiny, cup-like nest from 3 to 30 feet high on the downward sloping branches of an apple, beech, birch, hemlock, maple, oak, pear or sweet gum tree. The more western rufous hummingbird will nest in bushes, ferns, and dead, lichen-covered trees. Both are attracted by plantings of deep-throated flowers such as columbine, day lily, hawthorn, larkspur, lupine, trumpet vine and wild roses as well as commercial hummingbird feeders.

JUNCO

Usually preferring to nest beneath a brush pile, the roots of a fallen tree or an overhanging bank in a coniferous forest or wood-land roadside area, the junco is easily attracted to landscaped areas and gardens in the winter. It can be encouraged by seeds and nutmeats scattered on the ground, birch tree clumps, or a natural weedy patch of amaranth, burdock, smartweed, sunflower and this-tle. They also are fond of ragweed.

KINGFISHER

The kingfisher often appears in gardens near rivers or lakes. It always nests in a tunnel in a vertical bank usually overlooking and never very far from water.

KINGLETS

Kinglets usually nest in evergreen forests, but can take up residency in a garden with a dense evergreen patch. If lucky enough to have one nest in your yard, be cautious about going near the nest site as they are very shy and will leave if they feel the nest has been discovered. They are valuable additions to a garden because of their ability to glean insects, larvae and eggs from finer portions of trees.

MALLARD

The mallard or wild duck usually nests in thick cover on the ground near water. Sometimes it nests above the ground in a pollarded willow or tree stump. Mallards take readily to raised nesting boxes, in which they are much safer from predators.

MEADOWLARK

The ground-nesting meadowlark, though usually inhabitant of fields and meadows, may occasionally nest in a garden near fields if a lawn area is left unmowed.

MOCKINGBIRD

Excellent mimic and songster, the mockingbird sings while perched, in flight, and even at night. It is almost omnivorous, but favoring fruits and berries. It can be attracted to your yard by plantings of fruiting shrubs and vines. It usually nests from 3 to 10 feet high in dense shrubbery, hedges, low trees or viney tangles often close to a house. Nesting plants include barberry, blackberry, flowering crab apple, grape, greenbrier, hawthorn, honeysuckle, matrimony vine, multiflora rose, nannyberry and Russian olive. The fruits of these plants are all used for food, as are cherry, dogwood, elderberry, hackberry, holly, inkberry, and mulberry. Raisins, currants, nutmeats and apples can be offered at winter feeders.

MOURNING DOVE

Doves build crude open platforms of twigs in small trees or shrub hedges when available, although they will also nest on the ground. Being early nesters, they often build in cedars, hemlock hedges, hollies, rhododendron or other evergreens as well as young oaks and locusts or, in western states, Russian olive.

NUTHATCHES

Both the white-breasted and red-breasted nuthatches will nest in bird boxes as well as naturally-occurring tree holes or ones made by woodpeckers. They neatly plaster up the entrance hole with mud or pitch to the exact size they need. While the white-breasted nuthatch seems to prefer birch and apple trees, the red-breasted frequents conifers. Both of these birds can easily be attracted by winter feeding and will stay to glean insects from your tree trunks.

ORIOLES

The Baltimore oriole's hanging nest usually swings from the drooping twigs of an elm or weeping willow. Orchard orioles fasten their nests to the slender twigs at the top of an apple or other fruit tree. Western Bullock's orioles attach their nests to the branches of box elders, cottonwoods, mesquite or oaks. All are basically insectivorous though cherries and grapes may be taken at times. All appreciate an offering of short strings, bits of yarn and hairs at nest-building time.

OWL, BARN

As its name suggests, the barn owl prefers barns and old buildings for nesting purposes, where it nests on a flat surface such as a beam. It will also nest in the large hollow cavities often found in elms. It will sometimes occupy a nest box if this is suitably positioned in a quiet place, high in a tree or ivy-covered wall.

PHEASANT

Like the bobwhite, pheasants will come into a garden to nest, using man as protection against some of the sitting pheasant's many enemies.

PINE SISKIN

These birds, as their name implies, prefer cone-bearing trees such as the white pine, both for food and nesting sites. Feeder foods attractive to these rather tame visitors include hemp, millet and sunflower seeds.

PURPLE MARTIN

The martin, largest of the swallow family, is a highly beneficial insect-eating bird. It is colonial in nature and within its range will nest in large multiple-room houses. (See pp 69–70) A water source is an inducement to nesting as well.

RED-WINGED BLACKBIRD

Since they nest in colonies in grass tussocks or shrubs near water, it is not likely that these birds will nest in your garden. Lacking sufficient natural nest sites, an uncut grassy patch, cat-tails, or shrubs such as red-osier and willows around a pond will attract them. They are attracted in summer to mulberries and other fruiting plants, but in winter will gladly eat breads, seeds and grain such as cracked corn.

ROBIN

The robin is a familiar bird in city parks, suburban gardens, rural areas, and even woodlands. It will nest on a tree branch or crotch, in shrubs, under eaves, or on a nesting platform. Trees preferred for nesting include apple, cedar, cherry, dogwood, flowering crab apple, hawthorn, hemlock, maple and oaks. Dense mixed shrub borders of barberry, forsythia, lilac, spiraea and viburnum are also attractive, especially if located near a lawn area where earthworms can be obtained.

RUFOUS-SIDED TOWHEE

This large, ground-feeding sparrow is usually seen scratching and kicking on the ground beneath shrubbery in search of insects and seeds. A reliable source of food provided near shrubbery will often encourage nesting in your garden and year-round residency. Nesting is on the ground concealed in leaves, in a clump of grass, beneath a bush or hedge, or low in a thick bush such as barberry or maple-leaved viburnum.

SPARROWS

The majority of the sparrows which can be found in your garden during the winter will not be year-round residents as they breed in far northern areas. Probably the most widespread and most likely to nest in your garden would be the chipping sparrow, field sparrow or song sparrow. All of these may decide to nest in honeysuckle, multiflora rose or Virginia creeper tangles. The field sparrow is often attracted by an uncut grassy patch wherein it may hide its nest at the base of a clump of grass. It also may nest low in blackberry or chokeberry. While the song sparrow has wide-ranging nest habits which include nesting on the ground, in weed or grass clumps, or low in bushes, the chipping sparrow usually seeks dense cover, even nesting in evergreens. Both of these birds are attracted by the same bushes, which include, in addition to those previously mentioned, barberry, blackberry, coralberry, forsythia, highbush blueberry, lilac, spiraea and the viburnums. Nearly all of the sparrows can be attracted in winter by natural patches of weeds and grasses or offerings of mixed bird seed, cracked corn, sunflower seeds, bread crumbs, cornmeal, dry cereals, nutmeats, raisins and berries, preferably strewn on the ground.

Starling

This cavity-nesting bird will nest in holes beneath roof guttering, in chimneys or any suitable crack or cranny in a building. It will also nest in tree-holes or nest boxes, often evicting the occupant. Although they tend to compete for nest sites with the more desirable bluebirds, martins and woodpeckers, they will glean tremendous numbers of grubs from your lawns.

Swallows

These birds are not only cavity-nesters, but masons as well. Most construct nests of mud and straw under the eaves of buildings, on sides of garden sheds or garages, or on nesting platforms. Since they are exclusively insect-eaters, they are welcome additions to any garden. Though plantings will not attract them as residents, a garden pool, mud hole, supply of dried grasses or straw, and provision of ledges along outbuildings will encourage their nesting.

Tanagers

Brightly colored tanagers usually nest in trees, anywhere from their lower branches to the very tops where they often feed upon such insects as caterpillars, bark beetles, gypsy moths and wood borers. Western tanagers prefer aspen, fir, pine and spruce forests, while the scarlet tanager of the East frequents deciduous or pine-oak woodlands. Summer tanagers in the South nest in pine-oak woods as well, while in the Southwest they utilize cottonwood and willow for nesting.

Thrushes

Closely related to the robin, the thrush has similar nesting habits though it prefers gardens bordering on a woodland area. The veery

85

prefers a moister habitat than other thrushes and it also nests lower to the ground.

TUFTED TITMOUSE

These alert, gray tufted birds can become welcome year-round residents in your garden. Their nesting habits are similar to those of the chickadee. Both birds will repay winter feeding of suet, sunflower seeds, bread, mixed seeds, nuts, raisins and berries by consuming large numbers of caterpillars, plant lice, bark beetles, wasps and other garden pests.

VIREO

The various vireos usually suspend their nests from crotches of thin branches in saplings or from the lower branches of an apple, birch, cherry, dogwood, maple, oak or poplar. Some species will nest in mixed shrub borders containing forsythia, lilac, spiraea or viburnums if there is deep shade or a forest nearby where they can obtain insect foods.

WARBLERS

The many species of warblers cover a broad range of nesting habits. Each species has a particular preferred nesting habitat although the majority nest on or within 10 feet of the ground. Hence low-growing shrubs such as blueberry, cotoneaster and the cranberry as well as evergreen ornamentals afford nest sites and cover. The Parula warbler which builds a nest of Spanish moss high in a tree is an exception, as is the blackpoll, the Blackburnian, black-throated green, magnolia, myrtle and pine warblers which nest in cone-bearing trees. The chestnut-sided warbler and the yellow warbler are the warblers most likely to nest in low trees, hedges or ornamental shrubs such as barberry, forsythia, lilac, red-osier, spiraea and viburnums bordering a garden area. Yellow-breasted chats may nest in your garden if it has a secluded thicket of multiflora rose, a viney tangle or a berry patch, while the yellowthroat finds hedges near water suitable for nesting in or beneath. Although they are quite particular about nesting areas, almost any of the warblers may be migratory visitors to your garden in search of insect food.

WAXWINGS

Being dependent upon berries as food for their young, the waxwings are late nesters (June-September). Voracious fruit- and berry-eating birds, they are attracted to gardens planted with fruit- and berry-bearing trees and shrubs. Since nesting is usually on horizontal limbs of saplings and higher bushes in fairly open areas, the waxwing will come to a well-planted garden which has isolated shade trees such as apple, cherry, maples and Russian olive with berry-bearing shrub borders. They are known to be gregarious in winter (give them berries, cut-up fruit and raisins at the feeder) and are arch enemies of cankerworms in the summer.

WOODPECKERS

Nearly all of the woodpeckers bore nestholes in large branches or tree trunks, being especially fond of old apple trees, birches, cottonwoods, elms, oaks, pines and willows which provide plentiful insect food as well. They will sometimes utilize telephone poles or fence posts and may be attracted to a nest box if your yard lacks old trees. The small, downy woodpecker is probably the most common garden visitor and is easily attracted in winter by suet.

WRENS

Wrens, too, are valuable insect-eating birds which can be encouraged to nest in your garden by provision of proper nest boxes, although they may just as readily nest beneath the eaves of buildings, in drain pipes, old tin cans, or even a piece of laundry hung on a line.

CHAPTER FIVE

Food, Water, Perches and Roosting

FOOD AND FEEDING TECHNIQUES

So much has been written in detail about feeding birds on bird tables that it is not necessary to go into the subject except in broad outline.

Perhaps the main problem with bird feeding is to prevent all the food being eaten by the birds that we wish to discourage, namely English sparrows and starlings which will clear a bird table and eat the special and sometimes quite expensive food in a very short time. It is upsetting to see such birds gobbling up all the sunflower seeds while chickadees, titmice and nuthatches sit hungrily by.

To attract the more interesting wild birds it is absolutely essential that the food supply should be constant. If the English sparrows eat all the food within a short time of it being put out, it is unlikely that the more interesting birds will come to the feeding place, because the latter visit the garden only once or twice a day. If they find food always available their visits will become much more frequent, but if they find nothing they will go elsewhere. It is quite surprising how the titmice, chickadees, nuthatches, pine siskins, goldfinches, cardinals and grosbeaks appear when they find a constant supply of nuts and seeds.

English sparrows on the other hand stay in a very restricted area, keep a sharp eye on any place where food is put out regularly and are on the spot immediately. They work in conjunction with starlings, virtually monopolizing most bird tables.

To keep the sparrows and starlings away is quite a problem, but it can be overcome to a certain extent by taking advantage of the fact that sparrows and, to a lesser degree, starlings, are by nature extremely wary and cautious. Although they can become very tame at times, they can quickly become equally wild if properly scared once or twice. The feeding platform and food containers should be placed within, say, a foot and a half of a house window. Sparrows will soon descend to the platform and start to clear up the food. When the platform is well monopolized by them, a newspaper should be suddenly banged on the window pane by a person concealed behind the curtain. If this is repeated several times sparrows will become very wary of the feeding table and will depart to some place where they can eat their food undisturbed, whereas birds such as finches, cardinals, chickadees, titmice and jays will soon grow accustomed to being watched through a window at very close quarters and come readily to the table provided, of course, that the window is closed.

Most bird tables are put too far away from the house, on the false supposition that birds will be too frightened to come near the house. The great advantage of putting the table near a window of the house is that a really first-class view can be obtained of the birds visiting the table, and the table can be replenished from time to time merely by opening the window.

The food for a bird table should consist mainly of stale bread and cake crumbs, cooked potatoes, cooked bacon rinds, bits of fat or meat, bones, nuts, acorns, raisins, apples, sunflower seeds, canary seed, millet, potato chips, stale breakfast cereals, rice, cracked corn and crushed dog biscuits. Mealworms are the greatest delicacy, although these are expensive unless home-bred. However, many birds may become finger tamed with the aid of them or other favored tid-bits plus lots of patience!

To breed mealworms, find a coffee can or other covered metal container and puncture the lid with holes to provide ventilation. Then place a damp cloth or paper toweling on the bottom of the tin and cover it with a thick layer of oatmeal. Add cut-up raw potatoes to provide moisture, and some slices of bread (in which the eggs are laid). Cover this with a second layer of cloth, adding more oatmeal, bread and potatoes. Repeat this process until the tin is nearly full. Then put in a few hundred mealworms, keeping the tin always at room temperature.

After a few weeks the mealworms will turn into pupae and eventually into black beetles of the type which used to be seen all too often in old-fashioned bakeries. The beetles will lay eggs in the bread and their eggs will hatch into mealworms. Fresh potatoes and oatmeal should be added regularly.

It needs a certain amount of enthusiasm to breed mealworms successfully, but they are such a popular bird food that it is worth a try, especially if a warm, dry cellar is available.

One of the problems of feeding soft bills is that the bigger birds such as blackbirds are apt to fly off with a large piece of food and try to eat it elsewhere. Often the food is lost in undergrowth or taken away by members of the crow tribe. When snow is on the ground, it is invariably lost. To prevent this happening, it is best to devise some sort of feeder. One type has a wooden lid which fits on to a prism-shaped frame, covered by medium-sized mesh (about 1¼ in.) wire netting. It is attached to the feeding table by wire struts at each corner and can easily be removed for cleaning purposes. Such a feeder can obviously only be used for bulky house scraps.

Food containers for titmice, finches, chickadees, siskins and nut-hatches should hang free from a horizontal bar attached to a clothesline or tree limb within view of a window, as the antics of these birds are amusing to watch. As with all feeding containers, they should be suspended sufficiently high to be out of the reach of predators. Several smaller feeders are preferable to one large feeder as these birds are a bit shy and the larger, more aggressive species may monopolize a feeder, forcing these birds to go elsewhere. Many small, suitable birdfeeders are for sale in feed stores, pet departments and from catalogues. However, a simple, inexpensive and equally as effective feeder can easily be made from a large, metal juice can. Cut half way around each end with a can opener and fold the cut portions back into the can, thus concealing the sharp edges. Paint the outside a dull color and hang by threading wire or cord through one end and out the other.

Shredded coconut should not be given as it swells inside the bird. Peanut butter is best avoided, though many authorities recommend its use. Even when mixed with seeds, it may cause suffocation if it lodges in the throat of a bird. If used, it should only be in small amounts as a binder for other foods. Peanut hearts are liked by many birds and may be a more satisfactory form of this nut. Suet cakes of seeds and nuts are very satisfactory and there is little waste from this food form.

Mourning doves are now fairly common winter residents in most of the United States. They are mainly seed-eating birds but they will eat bread. In the summer they feed upon weed, grass and garden flower seeds, but since they are ground feeders, winter snows create problems for them. Scattering seeds and crumbs beneath shrubs and evergreens is helpful. Cracked corn is their favorite winter food and it is a good plan to buy a sack of it to feed these attractive birds, although it is hoped that they will not multiply to the extent that they become a nuisance.

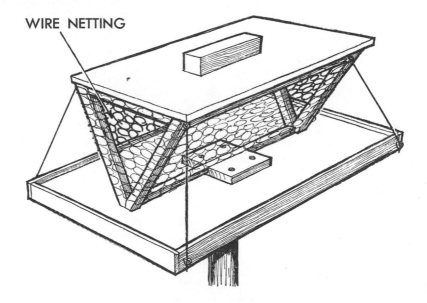

WIRE NETTING

Wire mesh feeder for the bird table.

Attracting woodpeckers to the garden is sometimes difficult unless there are several large trees and preferably some dead ones standing about. Providing suet feeders in several places will keep woodpeckers about for observation. Chunks of suet should never be placed directly on the bark of live trees as oils from it can damage living tissue. Split logs with rough textured bark make good feeders since the suet can be wired to them instead of the living tree and the rough bark provides a good surface to which the birds may cling. Hang these securely so winter winds do not cause them to swing about, frightening the birds. Open mesh bags, similar to the kinds turkeys and fruits sometimes come in, may be filled with suet chunks and hung from tree limbs. These are favored by the downy and hairy woodpeckers, chickadees, titmice and nuthatches.

Some birds such as cardinals, red-winged blackbirds and grosbeaks are not agile enough to cling to food containers and prefer their food on a table. This should be a simple wooden tray, preferably with a feeder, fixed on top of a wooden or metal post in such a way that mice, rats, cats and squirrels cannot climb on to it. The table should slope very slightly to allow water to drain off through a gap in the lowest corner. A roof over the bird table is quite unnecessary because birds always like to have an unobstructed field of vision when eating. Many bird tables are made with a roof over them, presumably to keep the food dry, but even so they usually get wet because the rain drives in at the sides.

Birds such as towhees, fox and white-throated sparrows, seem to prefer to take their food on the ground. These birds will usually hop round underneath the bird table eating the minute particles of food which fall on to the ground. For these dainty feeders it is advisable to scatter finely-crumbled bread or crushed seeds on the ground. English sparrows will not bother with these small particles if they can get hold of something bigger.

Feeding in Thick Snow

Birds can stand a very low temperature provided they can get enough food. Their metabolism is rapid and small birds have to eat about a third of their weight per day to maintain it at a correct level.

Most birds build up a certain fat reserve during the autumn months and this reserve is sufficient to tide them over short periods of very severe weather; but if the weather is very cold with heavy snow, and lasts over a week, many birds, particularly the ground feeders, may die of starvation. The stronger birds fly around in search of berries and will soon come to gardens. They are all very hungry and some of them will be tame enough to come to the table, while others such as towhees, waxwings, thrashers, thrushes and some sparrows will hang about looking rather miserable in the snow at the end of the garden.

This is the time to make a second feeding place by clearing away an area of snow, either on the lawn or in an open place away from trees if possible. Put out fruit, especially apples. It is often possible to purchase damaged fruit cheaply in food stores. Boil up any doubtful-looking potatoes and throw out all scraps, including chicken carcasses. In coastal areas seagulls may take a great deal of the food, but to some extent this can be avoided by dividing the food as finely as possible as seagulls like to pick up large pieces and make off with them. A herring gull can swallow a chicken drumstick in midair without difficulty. It is a good idea to cover up such a feeding site at night with sacks; then, if it snows again, the sacks can be easily removed with the snow on them, thus keeping the feeding place clear. Beware of attracting predators which might prey upon the birds you have attracted.

Birds such as crows, magpies and blue jays usually manage to find enough food even in the coldest weather, as they will prey upon sick and injured birds or animals as well as feed upon dead ones. These same birds have adopted an interesting technique for getting a meal easily. They wait until a bird with a piece of food in its beak flies away from a bird table. They then dive-bomb the poor bird until it gives up its food and has to go back for more, when the process is repeated.

FEEDING IN FROSTY WEATHER

In very frosty weather, some birds, particularly towhees, thrushes, fox sparrows and white-throated sparrows, find a lot of food by turning over leaves, the insulating properties of which keep the underlying ground free from frost and allow insects and worms to be found. It is therefore a good idea to allow fallen leaves to remain beneath shrubbery since they do help provide food for insect-eaters as well as enrich your garden soil.

Birds which are insectivorous, such as warblers, vireos, robins, thrushes, orioles, tanagers and fly-catchers, don't have much difficulty in getting sufficient food during the winter provided there is no severe frost or snow. Many of these birds stay out in the open countryside away from buildings as long as the weather is favorable. If a severe frost or storm comes, they will move into backyard gardens looking for food. This is when they are in real need of a meal and they may eventually come to the bird feeders. It helps to have a supply of raisins, berries, cut-up fruits and suet for these birds.

Seed-eating birds such as a goldfinch, pine siskin, purple or house finch, cardinal, junco or sparrow, are not real hard-pressed for food unless there is a heavy fall of snow which covers up all plant seed heads. Birch trees, since they hold their catkins into winter, are a valuable natural food supply during frosty weather; however, supplementary feeding will insure the survival of these birds. Any of a variety of seeds, or a combination of any of the following may be used: millet, hemp, rape, canary seed, milo, wheat, hulled oats, buckwheat, flax, cracked corn, peanut hearts and sunflower seeds.

Unwelcome as they may be, the English sparrows are usually the first birds to appear at the feeding table. Their appearance, however, is a signal to other birds that food is available. Consequently starlings, grackles, red-winged blackbirds, blue jays, mourning doves and other sparrows soon appear. In time the cardinals, finches, siskins, grosbeaks, nuthatches, titmice, chickadees and redpolls will appear. It is a good idea to provide additional feeders about the garden for the less aggressive birds as they appear. Another trick is to toss some bread crumbs, table scraps, cracked corn, millet and suet on the ground in an open but out-of-the-way portion of the garden. Soon the sparrows, starlings, grackles and red-wings which are more fond of ground feeding will gather in that place and leave the feeding table free for song birds.

NATURAL FOOD IN WINTER

As birds require a source of food which can act as an emergency supply when their normal food is not available, it is wise to plant shrubs and trees which are late fruiters rather than those which fruit in August and September when the food supply is plentiful. The berries of the hawthorn undoubtedly provide much winter food for robins, thrushes, cardinals, catbirds, grosbeaks, redwings and waxwings. It is obvious that if these trees are cut back every year there will be no berries, and unfortunately this is what is happening to our roadside hedges. Anyone who has a free-growing hawthorn in his garden will have a good supply of winter food for garden birds.

The berries of all types of holly tree are eaten during very cold spells by the thrush family, but they seem to be less popular than the berries of the hawthorn. Cotoneaster berries will remain on the branches until the severe weather sets in, and such berries are very attractive to waxwings. It is interesting to watch these sociable birds pass berries from one to another as they sit about in the branches of berry-bearing garden shrubbery and trees. Pyracantha berries ripen in September, but as they are very popular with some birds there are often not many left when the severe weather appears. Crab apple trees are, of course, very useful, and the fallen apples will often last a long time on the ground and will be eaten by the thrush family and mockingbirds. The mountain ash is always a reliable fruiter, but its September berries have usually disappeared before Christmas. The dogwood also is usually picked clean shortly after the first frost. However birch, box elder, hackberry, oak, Russian olive and sour gum provide long-lasting supplies of winter foods. Most weed seeds will be eaten by the goldfinches, house finches, purple finches, pine siskins and juncos. Such seeds are supplied by dock, plantain, chickweed, thistle, shepherd's purse, teasle, ragweed, goldenrods and the many wild grasses. The seeds of garden flowers will also be eaten. Some of the flowers which produce attractive seeds as well as lovely blooms are columbine, phlox, pinks and salvia; and annuals such as gaillardia, larkspur, marigolds, petunias, snapdragons, verbena and zinnias.

ALL-THE-YEAR-ROUND FEEDING

It is generally not necessary to feed birds all the year round, except in very built-up areas and in dry weather, when insectivorous birds cannot get enough food for their young. Those of us who have the time and interest, however, to put out a regular supply of mealworms, will be well rewarded because birds will become almost finger tame and completely trusting in the person who puts out their daily supplies, even though they will still retain their inborn fear of any other person.

WATER

Birds use water both for drinking and for bathing. Most garden birds like bathing—the starling in particular will take a bath however cold the weather is. Some birds, such as game birds, have a dust bath to clean their feathers, as will sparrows, robins and jays. Birds never soak themselves completely, but dampen the ends of their feathers and then, using the oily substance from their preening gland, they clean each feather individually, particularly the flight feathers. They use the most ingenious antics to get the oily substance on to the parts inaccessible to the beak.

The ideal bathing and watering place for birds is a shallow cement pond holding not less than 15 gallons of water, so that the risk of drying up is lessened. Shallowness at one end is highly important. Small birds like a depth of only about ½ inch and larger birds a depth of 1–2 inches so that the pond should have a very gradual slope.

Once a bird has established a habit of drinking at one particular place, it will come regularly several times a day as long as the water supply is adequate. One method of keeping the water supply constant is to connect the drain pipe which drains the rain water off a shed or garage, to the pond. By this means, except in very dry spells, the pond will remain well filled up.

The site of the pool is very important. It should be in fairly open ground in the sun, and not too close to any shrubs which may conceal a cat. The north end of the pool should have a small bank facing squarely to the south. In very cold weather, when the pond is frozen hard, the ice will thaw at the edge under this bank by midday, if there is any sun about, and will provide a valuable source of water for the birds. The location of the shallow end does not matter provided it is not in a dip, which would prevent the birds from keeping a sharp look out for enemies while drinking and bathing. A well-appointed pool is a great asset to any garden and gives a center of interest. Birds seem to be attracted to water in the same way as we are. Whether because of the aquatic flies and beetles which frequent small ponds or whether it is because they use it as a sort of meeting place, it is impossible to say.

A finely-set lawn spray will always attract the birds which like bathing. If used during long, hot, dry spells it will act as a substitute for rain and, in addition, it will bring worms to the surface.

Plastic pools are easy to put in, but are generally not very attractive to birds because they cannot get a proper grip with their claws, as they can on cement; but if small stones of about 2½ inches in diameter, which don't slip about easily, are carefully laid on the bottom creating a shallow depth, the birds will be able to obtain a better grip while bathing. Ornamental baths again are unsatisfactory, because they are usually small and dry up too easily, thus needing constant attention.

Birds require water during long, frosty spells when the ground is dry and hard, but when there is snow they quench their thirst with the small amounts of snow which stick to whatever food they eat. Chickens will always eat snow if they cannot find their water trough. A straw-filled sack placed over a corner of the pond on top of a board will help to stop the ice becoming very thick, or may even stop it freezing. A more certain method of stopping water freezing is to use a thermostatically-controlled immersion heater of the type used for aquaria. The container should be made of poor heat-conducting material, such as asbestos or plastic, and sunk into the earth to avoid heat loss. A pyramid-shaped rough stone should be put in the middle to prevent small birds from drowning themselves. Specially made drinking containers, with heating mechanism attached, can be purchased.

PERCHING POSTS

When a bird flies round the garden it usually goes to certain favorite perching places in various trees. These are used as singing places and also as vantage points to see if all is clear before flying elsewhere. Many male birds often have three or four singing posts round the nest, using each in rotation to issue his warning to rival birds to keep out of his territory. Robins, blue jays, flycatchers, grosbeaks and mourning doves are all birds which have their favorite perching places in a garden. It is therefore a good idea to fix up an artificial perch in the shape of a T by using a rustic pole about 6

Food, Water, Perches and Roosting

feet high with a short transverse pole on top. The best place to put it is near the drinking pool, where birds will use it as a preliminary perch to see that all is clear before they go down for a drink. If there are flycatchers about they will almost certainly use the perch, and will provide a good display of their aerial acrobatics from such a post. During the night, owls are very likely to use it as a perch from which to watch for mice. It is the simplest thing to construct and will make it possible to obtain a much better view of many garden birds.

ROOSTING PLACES

A sheltered and secure roosting place is essential for a bird's survival, and this applies more particularly during the winter months when a bird has to spend as much as 16 or 17 hours out of the 24 in its roost. During this time it is losing a great deal of body heat, especially in very cold weather. Birds will therefore choose a place where they are out of the cold wind and protected from rain. They sometimes need to alter their roosting site according to the weather or the direction of the wind, but usually as soon as the cold weather starts they select a communal roosting site permanently protected from north and east winds and with sufficiently thick evergreen foliage to keep off the rain and snow. They will use this roost throughout the winter, returning each day to their own special feeding grounds. As soon as nesting activities begin the cock bird roosts in a tree near his setting mate.

Most garden birds roost at least 6 to 9 feet from the ground and near the top of the tree so that they can fly out quickly if disturbed. They avoid using tall trees, as these would catch too much wind. The ivy-covered trunks of trees are popular roosting places because here the bird can change its position according to the prevailing wind. Clumps of shrubbery, hedges or thick evergreens about 9 feet high are also much used. Holly trees are quite popular, provided there are several trees together. Thick ivy growing on a south-facing wall is especially popular. Yew trees are less useful for roosting as the leaves are too small to keep off the rain. Certain types of cedars, junipers and arborvitae which have a very thick, vertical growth are almost weatherproof, and such trees are often used by sparrows and robins for roosting. Fir trees, such as the spruce, do not give suffici-ent wind protection unless they are grown in clumps. An evergreen

Perching posts are simple to
construct and are valuable
for bird observation.

which has big, strong leaves, such as a rhododendron, andromeda or
laurel, particularly if grown against a sheltered wall, will always be
popular as a roosting place. Bramble bushes provide very popular
roosting cover except during the winter months.

A bird always tries to avoid getting wet at night because it has no
chance of drying itself by flying about, and may lose so much body
heat if it gets really soaked that it can die of cold. If it is raining or
snowing when a bird goes to roost, it will get under a large leaf and
thus keep dry; but if it is windy as well, the leaves will be disturbed
and the bird will have an uncomfortably wet night. For this reason,
birds always select a roosting place well sheltered from the wind.

It is still sometimes believed that birds sleep in their nests. With a few exceptions, this is quite untrue, although wrens will roost together in old nests in order to keep warm, particularly if the nest is in a very sheltered spot such as on a wall, and owls will sometimes sleep during the day in their nest holes to avoid being mobbed by blackbirds and other garden birds. Sparrows, however, roost regularly in their old nests and also in nest boxes. In one nest box scheme, a third of the boxes in a count of 200 were used by sparrows for roosting.

Young swallows and purple martins, when they start learning to fly, will leave the nest for the whole day and will return to it again at night to roost. They will do this for perhaps ten days. It is therefore important not to pull down old nests too soon, particularly those of late-hatched nestlings which are often not ready to fly until mid-September when the weather can be quite cold and wet.

ROOSTING BOX

A roosting box can be made along the same lines as the standard bluebird box, but about twice as large. The hole, however, should be near the bottom and about 2½ inches in diameter. In addition, several dowel perches (⅜ inch by 4 inches) should be affixed in staggered positions within the box to prevent one bird from being directly above another. A small landing platform may be attached to the outside beneath the hole. Such a box should be erected in a sheltered area, preferably facing the south. Often several species of birds, usually cavity-dwellers, will roost together for added warmth and protection.

CHAPTER SIX

The Enemies of Birds

BIRDS HAVE MORE enemies than we perhaps realize, quite apart from the natural hazards of snow, severe frost, floods and, for some, the perils of migration.

The most dangerous time in a bird's life is when, as a fledgling, it leaves the nest. Its flight is weak and its perching ability not properly developed.

After leaving the nest, the young of most garden birds sit quietly for a few days, well concealed in a tree near the old nest, during which time their flight and tail feathers are growing rapidly. But if for some reason they are suddenly frightened, they scatter in all directions, some fluttering to the ground where they can fall an easy prey to a cat, rat or weasel. Others, being stronger, may perhaps manage to fly to another bush where they may survive, provided they keep off the ground. This scattering obviously causes much greater feeding problems for the parent birds and no doubt many young birds starve in this way.

Fledglings will also pop out of the nest a day or two before they would normally leave if they are disturbed by anything such as hedge-cutting or even by just being looked at. Once this has happened it is usually a waste of time trying to put them back in the nest, because they come out again. The best thing to do is to put

103

them in an open-fronted box with wire netting (chicken wire is usually suitable) across the front, putting the old nest inside. The box must be fixed firmly in the nesting tree or nearby, and it is most important to see that it is out of the reach of cats who will pull the whole box down if they can climb up to it. The young birds will be fed through the wire by the parents and after about five days, provided they appear to be in good shape, they can be released.

If young birds can survive this dangerous time in their lives, they are then faced with further enemies which unfortunately are on the increase. It is therefore essential for anyone interested in bird survival to understand something about the ways of these enemies as well as the hazards which we ourselves create.

MAN

From very early times, birds of all kinds have been netted and snared by man as a form of food, but their numbers were not noticeably depleted because the existing human population was small and only destroyed such birds as it needed to eat.

With the advent of the shot-gun things became very different. In the latter years of the nineteenth century there was a great craze for shooting rare and beautiful birds for stuffing, and many of our most attractive birds such as woodpeckers, kingfishers, goldfinches, cardinals, barn owls and many rare species were shot in order to satisfy this somewhat bizarre taste in ornaments. Plume hunters, also, slaughtered many thousands of birds for use in women's hats during this time. Fortunately this has stopped and many of the species with exotic plumage have been put under protection.

Birds of prey are still, unfortunately, persecuted in many parts of the country. Owls, hawks and eagles, including our national emblem, the bald eagle, are frequently shot on sight regardless of federal regulations. Farmers and ranchers may mistakenly blame these birds for destruction of domestic livestock. In actuality, the loss of a few lambs or chickens to predatory birds is certainly balanced by the thousands of rats, mice and rabbits which they capture. In fact, these birds are far superior to cats in keeping such rodents under control. Commercial fishermen persecute the osprey and eagle, yet these birds usually feed upon fish after spawning, when they would normally die anyway. Actually, the birds provide an invaluable clean-up service.

Probably more destructive than the outright killing of birds is man's drive for further development of the countryside. Uncontrolled building of more highways, industrial parks, shopping centers and housing developments combined with vast mechanized agricultural development has reduced much of the natural habitat to a mere remnant of what it once was. Without sufficient habitat, birds, as well as other animals, cannot survive.

The great progress in all branches of science is a potential threat not only to the lives of the lower creatures but to human lives as well—which is perhaps a good thing for, if we know we are all in it together, more care may be taken in future over how we apply our ever-expanding scientific knowledge.

POLLUTION

This is a subject about which much has been written recently in relation to the sea, rivers and agricultural land. It is hardly necessary to say that we must also be very careful about what we use in our gardens.

Man has already started to exploit nature, and in many instances the results of his exploitation have been not only unexpected but somewhat alarming. Biological processes are exceedingly complex and any exploitation has to work in the total context of the environment, namely man, animals, birds, insects, air, water, soil and plant life. Even a minor disturbance may produce a host of changes, both large and small. We cannot possibly foretell accurately from a laboratory experiment all the effects a certain chemical will have when it is used outside the laboratory in the complex environment of nature. When an error is made it can often be corrected, but this may not be before it has done severe and sometimes irreparable damage to living creatures, plants, insects or soil. Birds have been affected by the use of insecticides and sprays in several ways. Most obvious is that the killing of many kinds of insects greatly reduces the food supply of certain species of birds which in severe cases may lead to starvation. In some cases, the poisons kill not only insect pests, but also whatever wildlife, including birds, that live within the treated area. Some pesticides are cumulative, not causing immediate death, but gradually building up within the individual as successive contacts with the pesticide or pesticide-treated foods. The bird slowly dies as he ingests more and more of the chemicals. A more subtle effect is that several pesticides have been proven to create the inability to lay properly developed eggs, one which if widespread can lead to the extinction of a species within a relatively short time.

It is important to note that gardeners who make provision for birds have little need for pesticides as the birds themselves are an efficient means of reducing insect pests. In fact, the additional expense of providing for the birds is offset by not needing to purchase insecticides or needing to spend the time to apply them.

The alarming findings of excessive quantities of DDT even in polar bears and also in humans who have eaten fish and game and the possible cancer-forming properties of this chemical illustrate how we should not apply our scientific knowledge. An even more recent and equally alarming discovery is that a defoliant—2,4,5-T—used for killing brambles and undergrowth, causes death by paralysis of any living thing which gets a big enough dose; and, even worse, it has fetal-deforming properties.

Urbanization

As mentioned earlier, the encroachment of bricks and mortar into the countryside cannot fail to present a very serious threat to the livelihood of all birds except the starling and sparrow. Those who plan developments should not ban the growing of hedges round gardens or the erection of fences. It doesn't help the birds and it may be that it doesn't help us, either. Open-plan living is all right for some people but it can be carried too far, and psychologists say, not surprisingly, that we are far more prone to anxiety states and emotional disorders if we live too much on top of one another.

Those who plan highways and public parks should endeavor to plant trees which are useful to birds. The hawthorn, for example, is very cheap compared with other flowering shrubs, looks very colorful when grown as a standard tree in a public place and will certainly be used by garden birds for nesting. Its berries in the winter are an important source of food for resident birds and winter visitors. Clumps of hemlock, holly, pines and other evergreens should also be planted for protection against weather and for nesting and roosting.

Again, in most parts of the country road hedges are now trimmed by mechanical means. The tall, thick hedge in which a great number of birds regularly used to build their nests is now reduced to a thin little hedge in which no self-respecting bird will nest. Furthermore, hedge-trimming, weed-cutting and weed-spraying are now often carried out in the height of the breeding season, where formerly hedge-cutting and ditch-clearing were traditionally jobs to be done at the end of the season. There is no doubt that the new mechanical method of hedge-cutting has caused a vast reduction in the numbers of birds nesting in hedgerows.

THE AUTOMOBILE

An ever-increasing menace to all birds is the automobile. The number of birds killed on the roads each year runs into millions, according to a recent estimate. The greatest slaughter occurs in the early mornings of late spring and summer when birds fly on to the roads, probably to get grit and, not being fully alert after a night's roost, are killed by cars. It is frequently the young and inexperienced birds which succumb, for they have not had time to learn that a car is a highly dangerous machine. When birds are on the road, a quick toot on the horn will often save a life. Many people will not bother to do this and think it is of no matter to kill a few birds. They may even deliberately try to mow them down.

Quite apart from the death on roads caused by automobiles, the invasion of the countryside during the breeding season, particularly on weekends, by thousands of cars containing picnickers and day-trippers inevitably causes great interference with the successful breeding of birds. Bird photography has in the past done some harm where it has been pursued too enthusiastically, causing rare birds to forsake their nests, but improved equipment permits greater distance without sparing sharpness of detail. It has done a great deal of good by giving the public information about the more interesting and

107

intimate side of bird life. Bird-watching with binoculars is harmless enough when done by experienced people, but when parties of amateurs take to the countryside a great deal of disturbance can be inadvertently caused to bird life. It is unfortunate that it is always the rarest and shyest species which attract the most attention, and this must inevitably disturb the very birds which should be left in peace.

Motor boats, speedboats and helicopters are likewise invading the territories of birds who like solitude; and now, owing to the combustion engine, there are very few places left anywhere which are inaccessible to man. Such interference with nesting activities is serious, and more and more nature reserves must be created if we are to maintain the numbers of these rarer birds.

FOUR-LEGGED ENEMIES

Cats

The domestic cat probably originated from ancient Egypt and has been kept as a pet for centuries. In the United States, the cat is probably second only to the dog in popularity as a house pet.

Our domestic cat seems to enjoy the best of two worlds. It gets all the advantages of civilization—food, warmth and general protection from enemies—together with unrestricted, easy hunting whenever it wishes to satisfy its urge to kill. For cats are natural hunters and enjoy it. Some are good hunters and others are bad. They kill whether hungry or not and if they are not hungry they will play with their prey for some time before killing it. Female cats are usually the most efficient hunters and will kill rats, mice, weasels, rabbits and birds. They never restrict their killing to mice alone, as some people imagine, and they are thus a great deterrent to bird life in a garden. A cat prowling about at night makes all the birds uneasy and causes them to move elsewhere; and though the cat may catch only a few birds, it will reduce the number of bird visitors to a garden. Domestic cats which have gone wild and have to live off the country are a serious menace.

In the nesting season, cats will cause great destruction of bird life by both frightening the sitting bird off her nest at night and by killing off the young birds before or after they leave the nest. Cats find a nest quite easily by watching the parent birds going to and fro and they can climb any tree or shrub provided the branches will support their weight. They do not usually climb higher than 9 feet when hunting, as from this height they can safely jump to the ground in case of emergency—for it must be remembered that, when hunting, the domestic cat becomes almost a wild creature with all the instincts for self-preservation.

When a cat reaches a nest it will usually claw the nest over and tip out the contents. If it is full of young birds ready to fly this will add to the cat's entertainment.

Those who keep cats and let them out at night should remember that in built-up areas cats will wander from one garden to another, trespassing in the gardens of people who prefer birds to cats and generally creating a disturbance to bird life. A partial remedy for this is for cat lovers to let the cat out only during the day from mid-April till the end of July when the nesting season is at its height; if it is well fed, the cat will probably find a sunny corner and go to sleep. A cat bell on a collar is quite useful, not because it gives a warning to the birds, but because it puts the cat off its hunting. Just as the cat is making a silent spring on its prey, the bell gives an unexpected tinkle, which must be very annoying to an animal which relies so much on the element of surprise in its hunting tactics.

The best way to keep cats out of a garden is to use 2-inch mesh wire netting. For a hedge about 6 feet high, it would be necessary to use netting only 3 feet wide, which should be placed along the bottom of the hedge and pushed well in so that the twigs grow through the wire and cover it up.

Cats can jump a 6 foot wall if they can get a run at it. A length of wire netting about 18 inches wide put along the top of a wall or fence will stop them getting over. They can easily be prevented from climbing smaller trees by an encircling wire stop or metal sleeve around the trunk. Cats climb by embracing the trunk closely with their front legs and pushing up with their hind legs. Thus they cannot let go with their front claws for more than a fraction of a second, and if they try to circumvent any obstacle in their upward path they will certainly fall.

Dogs

It is rare for dogs to become destroyers of nesting birds. Labradors, with their keen scent and voracious appetite, may occasionally find and devour the eggs of a sitting pheasant or other ground-nesting bird but, generally speaking, dogs are not interested in hunting birds in the way cats hunt birds. Garden birds realize this and are therefore not unduly worried by the presence of dogs from a nesting point of view, knowing that there is less likelihood of cats being around if there is a lively, yapping dog in the garden. A dog of the terrier breed will tend to keep away ground predators such as foxes, weasels, rats and mice.

Dogs will usually avoid areas sprinkled with a fox repellent, and it is therefore wise to use this mixture where there are nests on the ground.

Unfortunately, in a garden where there are dogs (and, likewise, small children), birds are unlikely to become tame because they are disturbed if they see anything rushing around. Puppies, for instance, will often make a sally at a blackbird or mourning dove feeding on the lawn, just for the fun of it. Sudden, unexpected movements make birds more wary.

Foxes

There are many more foxes about than we realize, but since they have retained their nocturnal habits, we rarely see them unless we get up very early in the morning and keep a special watch in a likely area. In outlying suburbs, where they are not persecuted, they may have even increased in number. In some areas, foxes may be quite numerous and breed unmolested living on mice, rats, chickens, birds, rabbits and garbage.

There is no doubt that in the nesting season eggs and young birds form quite a considerable part of the fox's diet. When there are hungry cubs to feed and no rabbits about, a fox will take a bird incubating her eggs from any nest within his reach, plus all the eggs or young. Being an agile climber he can get up to quite considerable heights, and may cause some incubating hens to forsake their nests by disturbing them at night, even if he cannot reach the nests.

Unfortunately there is very little one can do to keep foxes away. A fox can get over, under or through almost any barrier except a fox-proof fence, which is an expensive item. Some lights hanging from a tree at the end of the garden will probably keep a fox away quite effectively for a month. The position of the lights should be changed occasionally. Fox repellents, sprinkled round a nest, are useful. Anything which suggests a trap makes a fox very suspicious. Pieces of metal or tins hammered to a stake and placed near a likely entrance through a hedge may make a fox turn back. The metal should be handled periodically to keep the human scent on it. The fox is a good swimmer and water will not stop him from taking ducks nesting on islands in ornamental pools. He is also a master hypnotist, and can often make his prey come to him if he cannot catch it by his usual methods. Members of the duck and crow tribe are particularly fascinated by foxes, and if they see one behaving in a peculiar manner or in any trouble they will quickly be on the scene to inspect.

The curiosity shown by wild duck about foxes has led many to their destruction in the following way. A mongrel dog, which has the same shape and color as that of a fox, is trained to lure wild duck into a decoy or "pipe" which consists of a small stream covered over by wire netting arched over the top. The stream leads off the main feeding pond. The foxy-looking dog appears at the mouth of the decoy and then disappears into the decoy to re-appear further up, behind specially-constructed hurdles. The ducks, with their insatiable curiosity, swim into the trap and keep following as the dog repeats its act. Eventually the dog-handler appears behind them at the entrance of the "pipe" and drives the ducks towards the narrow, upper end where they are caught in a net. This method was first used in the seventeenth century for catching ducks for food, but is now used for banding purposes.

Actually, the fox presents only a minor threat to birds in the garden. It is only in the absence of their favorite foods, rabbits and rodents, that they may become a problem to the birds. It is far more satisfactory to permit a few wild rabbits to reside in the garden so that their offspring will provide sufficient food for the foxes, than it is to try to prevent the fox from appearing in the garden.

Gray Squirrels

The charming ways of these animals are in sharp contrast to their methods of getting a living. They hunt both on the ground and in the trees, and whenever they find a nest they may devour the contents, eggs or young. They also eat fruit, nuts and acorns and will readily rob a bird table or nest box if they can get into it.

Positive means can be taken to discourage these creatures if they have become pests. Squirrel-proof feeders are available which have sheet metal collars around their bases. The gardener may also place collars around those trees which are known to contain nest sites provided there are no overhanging branches of adjacent trees or shrubs which could provide a means of access. During early spring when natural food is scarce and when nesting is taking place, try providing acorns, peanuts, sunflower seeds or peanut butter and jelly sandwiches for the squirrels. A squirrel that is well-fed will be less likely to rob the nests of birds. Once natural foods become plentiful, squirrels will retreat to the tops of large oak and maple trees and seldom be seen until late winter.

Weasels and Mink

The weasel is a charming but ferocious little acrobat who will rob any nest he comes across either on the ground or in a tree. He kills vast numbers of rats and mice which otherwise might become plagues. Weasels therefore play a very important role in the balance of nature and should be left unmolested by man. Weasels usually breed twice a year but it is unlikely that their numbers would ever increase sufficiently to make them pests.

Escaped mink are now to be found in certain parts of the country. These creatures are fierce, uninhibited killers, destroying anything that lives in a tree or on the ground. An area unfortunate enough to be occupied by escaped mink will soon have very little wildlife left, for they kill for the fun of it as much as for food. Anyone who sees a mink should report it to the local conservation officer or game warden.

Rats and Field Mice

Both these animals are excellent climbers. The field mouse, a much bigger and more handsome fellow than the house mouse, is a robber of small birds' nests. Rats do not do a great deal of damage to tree-nesting birds because during the nesting season there is usually plenty of food on the ground and climbing exposes them to a certain risk. They would always take the contents of a nest built on the ground.

Field mice, on the other hand, spend a large part of their time climbing in hedges, bushes and even big trees. They often eat the eggs of birds and may sometimes convert the nest into one for themselves.

Raccoons

In some parts of the United States, there are relatively large populations of raccoons. They may be destructive to eggs and young birds, especially those of waterfowl and game birds. The best means of control is to provide as much cover as possible for your nesting birds. If the nests are well concealed, there is a good possibility that the raccoons will pass them up in favor of more obvious sources of food.

FEATHERED ENEMIES

Crows

The crow tribe in North America consists of ravens, crows, magpies and jays. Ravens, the largest of our "songbirds," are no longer as plentiful as they once were. Although a useful scavenger, they also will prey upon poultry and, for this reason, were persecuted widely; as a result their range has been reduced to the Far North and western states near heavy timber, and they are not of much concern to the bird gardener.

The common crow has spread throughout the United States, being found in great numbers near farming areas where they consume great quantities of insects, mice, rabbits and grain. Unfortunately, they also seem fond of birds eggs, although they are more of a menace to the eggs of ground-nesting birds such as game birds, waterfowl, meadowlarks, horned larks, bobolinks, and gulls than they are to smaller tree-nesting birds. Often crows can be seen in flight being harassed by smaller birds. During the winter, if food is scarce, great flocks of crows may invade garden feeders.

Magpies

Of all the crow tribe, the magpie is the most cunning and most destructive of bird life. It will take the eggs and young of any bird whose nest it can reach, and the only birds immune to its attacks are those that build in holes and crevices, such as starlings, woodpeckers, house wrens, chickadees and titmice.

In the United States, the magpie is confined to an area bounded on the east by the central and Great Lakes states and on the west by the Pacific Ocean. Ranging northward into Canada, the magpie is seldom seen south of northern Arizona or New Mexico. It usually frequents open areas near heavy brush or trees strong enough to support its large, platform nest. In areas where it is concentrated in large numbers, it is considered a pest as it will prey upon domestic birds, the young of sheep or cattle and domestic pets, as well as wild birds. It is omnivorous and functions well as an insect and rodent control, and scavenger, but this is often overlooked because of the damage it does.

It is reported that magpies often work with a fixed tactical plan. While the hen magpie is incubating her eggs, the cock goes off hunting for eggs and young birds. As a good burglar, he "cases the joint" before acting. This is done by sitting on a high tree and watching the comings and goings of nesting birds. Having marked down certain nests for destruction, he comes in very early in the morning when he can work undisturbed and quite fearlessly robs the nests he has marked, wherever they are situated. All this is done very quickly, without fuss or noise. Many birds do not give an alarm call as they would for jays or owls. Unless a person happened to be watching, he would probably be unaware of what had happened.

The cock magpie will not come back again for some days. He has plenty of other nests marked down for destruction. After about a week the birds whose nests have been robbed will have built again and there may be two or three eggs in the nests. These will again be taken. This goes on throughout the breeding season, the nesting birds providing food for the rapacious magpie.

Bird gardeners in the eastern and southern states are fortunate that they do not have to deal with a problem of this sort. For those that do, there is little that can be done other than destroying magpie nests to control the population of these birds. In an attempt to keep them away from a nest, it sometimes helps if a piece of black and white fabric, in imitation of a magpie, is hung up about 6 feet away from the nest.

Blue Jays

The blue jay is an attractive and common bird, especially in suburban or woodland gardens. Unfortunately his reputation as a nest robber is greater than he deserves. The slight destruction which he may cause is certainly compensated for by his function as a sentinel for the bird community. His familiar scream serves as a warning to all birds in the area that danger is near. He has thus saved many a bird from becoming the victim of a cat by giving warning in time for it to seek protective cover.

Other relatives, the Steller's jay and pinyon jay of the western states, will also rob nests of eggs and young. Since both of these birds frequent wilder areas, they are not too much of a problem to the home gardener. They may, however, often be winter visitors to garden feeders near areas where they reside.

English Sparrows

The cheerful, cheeky sparrow must unfortunately be numbered as one of the enemies of other garden birds because it is not only greedy and aggressive but also such an efficient, prolific breeder that it tends to keep other birds away by sheer weight of numbers.

English sparrows breed so successfully because they choose inaccessible nesting sites in buildings and raise as many as three broods a year.

Where food is concerned, they can live on an insectivorous diet or a seed diet. This gives them a great advantage over other garden birds, which are much more selective in their diet.

In addition, a sparrow, though only a small bird, is extremely strong physically, with a powerful beak and very well-developed flying muscles. It uses this strength to get what it wants.

Not only do sparrows monopolize the food supply, but also the nesting sites. They will evict purple martins from their apartments or harry a titmouse trying to build in a nest box. Sparrows have been seen pulling out a flycatcher's nest and also building on top of a swallow's nest, having first thrown out the eggs.

Sparrows have become parasitic on man and they are rarely seen far from buildings except during the harvest, when they settle in their hundreds on ripening grain. They are quick to learn, wary and suspicious, with a highly-developed sense of self-preservation. They are also to a certain extent parasitic on other birds. If, for example, they see a robin on the lawn with a tid-bit, several sparrows will arrive as if from nowhere, and if the tid-bit is to their liking they will take it.

Anyone therefore who wishes to have interesting birds in his garden should keep the sparrow population down as far as possible. The best way to do this is to block up all nesting holes in the house, wire over all drainpipes and destroy any nests. This is well worth doing, because one of the chief causes of blocked and broken drainpipes and damp walls is the sparrow's nest, which is often built in the swan neck of a roof drainpipe. When it rains heavily the nest is washed down the pipe. Another nest is then built and this suffers the same fate until there is a complete blockage of the drainpipe. If there is a severe frost the pipe splits and a great deal of expense can be involved in repairing or replacing it. Sparrows will also nibble away any loose mortar under a roof to make a nesting hole, and will pick the cement away from under the roof tiling at gable ends, thereby letting in the rain.

They are related to weaver birds and can, if necessary, build a domed nest in a tree. It can usually be recognized as a rather ragged yet highly efficient construction of dried grass, old bits of string, feathers, newspaper and any kinds of odd materials.

Sparrows are estimated to be now the most numerous bird in the world. They have spread north the arctic circle, and it is fascinating to think how they have adapted themselves to these extreme temperatures. In certain intelligence tests they have been rated equal to the white rat. There is certainly no danger of a sparrow shortage, however much we restrict their breeding activities.

Starlings

This bird, like the sparrow, owes its rapid expansion in many countries of the world to the fact that it always builds its nest in inaccessible places and can eat almost any type of food. Starlings always seem to be hungry; when food is put out on a bird table, not one or two starlings appear, but perhaps a dozen, and the food quickly disappears. Their voracious appetites and expanding numbers are likely to prove a menace to garden birds, especially in a dry summer when insectivorous food for young nestlings is scarce, but they certainly help remove grubs from a lawn area.

Although they have some pleasant characteristics, these birds should be discouraged. We have encouraged them quite long enough—for whenever we erect a new building we are, in fact, putting up an artificial nesting device for them, as well as for sparrows, usually at the expense of the more interesting garden birds.

Starlings are cavity-nesters and will build in any hole or chimney, but they never build a nest in the branches of a tree. They can cause considerable damage to houses by blocking up gutters and drains with their nesting material, and it is therefore a wise thing to stop up all holes and put wire over chimney tops.

Shrikes

Fortunately for bird gardeners, the shrikes, though spread throughout the country, are not especially common. These birds pursue insects, small birds and rodents with extreme skill. Since they prefer open country, they are not too likely to be found in thickly shrubbed suburban gardens.

Hawks

The Red-shouldered and Red-tailed hawks are the ones most often seen hovering over or perching near open pieces of ground watching for mice, rabbits and larger insects which form the main part of their diets. They will occasionally take birds if other food is difficult to find. They are, however, invaluable aids in controlling rats and other rodents in open fields, meadows and dumps. The sparrow hawk is both the smallest and most common of the falcons. It is frequently seen perching on poles and wires near open fields. Although it will eat sparrows and other small birds, its principal diet is grasshoppers. Actually, this tiny hawk does much to help prevent the extensive crop damage which could occur if the grasshopper population grew out of control. As such it is a benefactor and should be encouraged.

The peregrine falcon or duck hawk is probably the hawk which is most harmful to birds, as they make up the bulk of its diet. This fast-flying bird which usually dives upon its prey, has become rather rare, however. It frequents coastal areas, woodlands and mountain regions countrywide. The pigeon hawk, which has become rather uncommon also, is probably the most useful of the birds for keeping down the population of English sparrows, yet it is not large enough to prey upon poultry. Its varied diet includes shorebirds, songbirds to pigeon-sized, mice and insects. Also preying upon the smaller to pigeon-sized birds is the sharp-shinned hawk, a hawk which is essentially a woodland species. In addition it preys upon insects such as grasshoppers and moths, so it isn't purely harmful. The majority of other hawks may take birds from time to time, but their diet is primarily made up of rodents, rabbits, other small mammals and assorted insects, so they are, as a group, more beneficial than harmful. As such, they should be afforded as much protection as possible.

Owls

Many of the owls, the barn owl in particular, appear to be less common than they were. This again may be caused in part by the poisoning of rodents upon which the owls feed, or due to poison accumulations in the systems of those which feed primarily upon insects which have been subjected to various insect sprays. Barn owls and long-eared owls feed primarily upon small rats and mice though sparrows and other small birds may be taken when rodent food is scarce. Screech owls, barred owls and short-eared owls will take young birds as well as small rats, mice and beetles.

The harm done to birds during the nesting season is infinitesimal compared to the damage done by cats, squirrels and the magpie, and owls should be actively encouraged, as they kill off tremendous numbers of rodents.

Hawks and owls have been included in this section because people mistakenly regard them as a possible menace to garden birds. Their numbers being what they are and the fact that they do not frequent very populated areas, preferring large open spaces to the smaller suburban garden, does not make them much of a threat.

CONCLUSION

Bird Conservation

FOR MANY OF our rarer birds, the time has long since passed when they could survive on their own, without some form of special protection. The time will soon come when the more common birds of the woodland and garden will need protection, too, as the relentless destruction of their normal habitat continues.

This may sound like an alarmist call, but it is not; for if we continue at the current rate to encroach on the natural breeding grounds of birds, many species will suffer a severe decrease in their numbers. In brief, our many attractive garden birds are retiring slowly but surely before an army of sparrows and starlings who come like camp followers with the advance of man into the country-side. These camp followers are gregarious, and don't mind overcrowding. They are quick adaptors and sufficiently aggressive to take over new territory without any difficulty at the expense of the birds who lived there before.

The United States is rich in bird life and has a variety of habitats which continue to attract a great number and selection of birds. There are deciduous and evergreen forests, open fields and mead-ows, swamps, waterways and deserts, each with their own indigenous species which remain year-round to feed and raise their young. In addition, there are vast migratory routes and flyways in which birds travel. Birds fly southward from breeding grounds in northern states,

Canada, or even the arctic to wintering grounds in the south each fall. In the spring they return. In addition, birds from South America, Central America, Mexico and the southern states move northward for the summer and return in the fall. Thus the variety of birds which may visit your garden is not limited to those which are permanent residents. Migrating species may visit, and if they find circumstances to their approval, stay for prolonged periods. Of course, we cannot expect any birds to stay unless we make provision for them. If we can only realize that, unwittingly, man above all else is the greatest enemy of all his fellow creatures, then we are on the way to removing this very real threat to their existence. It is equally important to realize that man, if he understands the needs and habits of his fellow creatures, can, if he so chooses, be their greatest ally.

Fortunately, things are moving in the right direction. The teaching in schools on natural history has been extremely sensible and forward-looking and the younger generation takes a great interest in the subject. Excellent television films have unquestionably been a major factor in showing us the charm of birds and animals and has stimulated a healthy interest in them. There is now much more emphasis on preservation, and though shooting will always remain an outlet to satisfy the natural aggressiveness and pent-up frustrations of man, many restrictions and penalties are being imposed to prevent the extinction of rarer species.

Birds have a very strong instinct for survival and are quick to take full advantage of any favorable conditions that we create for them. The balance between survival and death is often quite small, and the factor for tipping the balance one way or the other is invariably due to the action of man. Bird populations are certainly affected adversely by prolonged and severe cold weather and by storms and other natural hazards during migration, but they can recover from such set-backs; given a few good breeding seasons the survivors, being fitter and stronger than those who succumbed, soon bring the numbers back to normal.

But the constant interference by man, as opposed to the intermittent interference by nature, is something with which birds cannot cope and it is bound to cause a decline in all bird populations except those of sparrows and starlings.

There is little we can do for the shyer and rarer species, or those which by choice or life-style live away from human habitation, except to create sanctuaries. Much has already been done in this direction but we still need many more with greater restrictions on entry by the public. The high price of land means that sanctuaries are often made where the soil is infertile, rocky and treeless— territory which can only be inhabited by ground-nesting birds. Our more familiar songbirds need a much more fertile environment with trees, hedges and cultivated land in order to breed successfully.

Those of us who are interested in bird survival can each make a definite contribution even if we have only a small garden, for there is nothing more certain than that, given the right conditions, garden birds prefer gardens and will thrive in them—giving us, at the same time, much pleasure.

A little private enterprise or "do it yourself," as opposed to leaving the problem to the powers-that-be, is essential if we wish to prevent what may be a common species today from becoming a rare one in the near future. We can most certainly help these birds and try to tip the balance in their favor not only by feeding them in bad weather but also by providing them with nesting sites, artificial or natural, and by seeing that they are left unmolested. The satisfaction of seeing a young brood of birds emerge safely from a purpose-built nesting site can be sufficient reward for all the work which has gone before. Difficulties and disappointments will arise despite every pre- caution, but this is the way of nature—and success is not worth having unless it is difficult to achieve.

NOTES:

Birds